ED Research Series

The Employment Department is committed to promoting a competitive, efficient and flexible labour market so that Britain can compete effectively within the European Community and in wider world markets.

The Department has policies and programmes in place to help to achieve this goal. For example, to ensure that unemployed and other disadvantaged people have the skills and motivation they need to compete actively for jobs; to help improve the skills of the workforce and entrants to it; to maintain a framework which provides a fair balance between the interests of people at work and their employers; to protect people at work from industrial risks; to encourage employment patterns, practices and attitudes which promote individual choice and enterprise; and to promote the interests of women in the workplace and beyond.

To ensure that public money is well spent we must continue to monitor the extent to which the Department is achieving its aim and objectives. To do this we need systematic and impartial information on the operation of the labour market and the Department therefore funds a comprehensive range of research and evaluation work to complement regular labour market statistics.

The Department's Research Series makes the findings of these studies publicly available as a contribution to discussion and debate on improving the workings of the British labour market.

Richard Bartholomew
Chief Research Officer

CONTENTS

LIST OF TABLES

Summary

- The aim of this project was to examine the employment characteristics of highly qualified women, to compare the occupational status and earnings of highly qualified women with highly qualified men, and to compare the employment situation and history, attitudes and domestic situation of highly qualified women with lower qualified women.

- For the purpose of this report, the highly qualified were defined as holding one or more of the following qualifications; university or CNAA Higher Degree of UK standard; university or CNAA First Degree or equivalent; teaching qualification (excluding degrees); nursing qualification (including SEN, SRN, SCM); Higher National Certification (HNC) or Diploma (HND), BEC, TEC, BTEC Higher Certificate or Higher Diploma, City and Guilds Certificate Full Technological, Part III (hereafter Higher BTEC/ City and Guilds equivalent); other higher technical, professional or higher qualification (where any of above are not held).

- Qualifications gained at university or from CNAA awarding institutions were defined as non-vocational or higher academic and the remainder of the list above as higher vocational. For coding purposes a higher level of qualification takes priority, such that someone with a degree and an additional higher technical qualification would be classified first as having a degree.

- A quarter of the BHPS sample of working age held qualifications above 'A'level GCE. Of these, 44% had a university degree or equivalent, 22% had a nursing or non-university teaching qualification, 23% held a Higher National Diploma, BEC/BTEC/TEC Higher Certificate or Higher Diploma, or Advanced or Final City and Guilds Certificate, and 12% had an 'other' higher vocational qualification. Men were marginally more likely to hold a degree, and substantially more likely to have BTEC/ City and Guilds or equivalent qualifications.

- Age shows a significant negative correlation with level of qualification, with a greater proportion of the sample under the age of 45 holding a higher qualification than the older group. Twice as many of the younger respondents held a degree or a BTEC equivalent qualification than did older sample members.

- Marital status is related to employment status for women with and without higher qualifications. Whilst three-quarters of non-married women were in full-time employment, under half of highly qualified married women had full-time jobs. Our sample of highly qualified men were, however, more likely to be unemployed or self-employed compared to their female counterparts, whilst women with degrees were twice as likely to be self-employed than higher vocationally qualified women. Married women with degrees were significantly less likely to be economically inactive than women with vocational qualifications, whilst for non-married women the proportions out of the labour force were similar. Married higher academically qualified women were less likely to work part-time than women with higher vocational qualifications.

- Overall, highly qualified men and women with degrees were equally likely to be in the top three occupational groups of SOC, comprising managerial or administrative, professional and associate professional occupations, but fewer women with vocational qualifications were in these occupations. Women in the professional occupations were substantially less likely to be in the science and engineering professions compared to men, the majority being found in teaching positions or associate health professions. Highly qualified men were more evenly distributed amongst the top three occupational groups, but more occupied corporate managers or administrators jobs. Very few highly qualified men and women were managers or proprietors in services or agriculture. Few highly qualified women were in lower status occupations, apart from a number in clerical or secretarial occupations, whilst significantly more of the higher vocationally qualified were in 'personal service' occupations. Of the few highly qualified men in lower status jobs, almost 1 in 10 of those with higher vocational qualifications were in skilled engineering trades.

- Highly qualified men were twice as likely to work in private firms or companies, the Civil Service or central government than highly educated women. Highly qualified women were most likely to have jobs in the local government or local education sector, whilst more vocationally qualified women worked for the National Health Service or in State higher education. A greater proportion of highly qualified women were in jobs which were mainly done by the opposite sex than were men with degrees. However, significantly fewer higher vocationally qualified women were in male dominated jobs.

- Of employees, women with higher vocational qualifications were least likely to have managerial duties but more likely to have supervisory responsibilities in their jobs. Male employees with degrees were most likely to have managerial duties whilst the proportions for higher vocationally qualified men and women with degrees were equal.

- On the whole, women with degrees were less likely than male higher academics to be in jobs which utilised their qualifications. However, generally speaking, both higher academic males and females were equally likely to be in jobs for which they were over-qualified. For the higher vocationally qualified, a different pattern was observed, where we found significantly more men than women in typically graduate level occupations. Of course, these patterns largely reflect the career choices of this group where women commonly chose to pursue nursing and teaching vocations. The majority of higher vocationally qualified women were in occupations matching their qualification, whilst higher vocationally qualified men were much more likely, than equivalent women, to be in low status jobs, for which basic or no formal qualifications were required.

- Women with teaching qualifications were far more likely to be currently in teaching posts than their male counterparts, but many more women than men with degrees chose teaching careers. Nursing qualifications were largely being used by men in their current jobs, whilst significantly more women with these qualifications were in lower status jobs. Men with BTEC/City and Guilds qualifications were significantly more likely than women to be in graduate level managerial jobs, but a large proportion of these men were also found in occupations generally demanding a lower level of qualifications than they held.

- The earnings from employment for highly qualified men were substantially higher than for women, with over a quarter more men than women in the highest earnings quartile. Higher vocationally qualified women earned significantly less than higher academically qualified women and their male counterparts. Furthermore, these patterns were evident regardless of age. Mean earnings from employment peaked in the middle age range for highly qualified women and higher vocationally qualified men, whilst for highly qualified men and vocationally qualified women earnings rose with age.

- Women with above 'A'level qualifications, and particularly those with academic qualifications, tended to be young, single and to have no dependent children when compared with women with lower qualifications.

- Highly qualified women were more likely to be in paid employment than those with lower qualifications. Where dependent children were present, highly qualified women were less likely to be in paid employment when compared with those holding similar qualifications who had no children.

- Highly qualified women who were in paid employment were more likely to be found in managerial, professional or associate professional occupations, to work full-time and to have higher earnings than those with lower qualifications.

- Within the sub-sample of all highly qualified women, there were marked differences in employment characteristics depending on the type of qualification held. Overall women with higher academic qualifications were more likely than those with higher vocational qualifications to hold professional, full-time jobs with relatively high levels of earnings when compared to all other women.

- Highly qualified women who were in paid employment were more likely to have opportunities for promotion and to have undertaken job specific training in the past year than those with lower qualifications which may be in part due to the career structures inherent in the occupations held by these women.

- Highly qualified women were more likely than lower qualified women to have been in continuous paid employment in the year previous to interview than lower qualified women. However highly qualified women, and in particular those with academic qualifications, were more likely than other women to have had more than one employment spell or more than one employer during the same period. This suggests highly qualified women may be more mobile within the labour market.

- Married or cohabiting women with higher qualifications tended to have spouse/partners with similar employment characteristics to themselves.

- Highly qualified women were less satisfied overall with their current job than lower qualified women, with the higher academically qualified being the least satisfied group.

- Highly qualified women were more likely than lower qualified women to give intrinsic rather than extrinsic reasons for working. However, the majority of all women gave the payment of essential household costs as their main reason for working regardless of the level of qualification held.

- Family responsibilities over the past year were less likely to have affected the employment of highly qualified women when compared to the lower qualified. Where highly qualified women did say their employment had been constrained by family responsibilities the main constraints given were childcare related. However, higher academically qualified women were also more likely to cite non childcare related responsibilities as having affected their employment than the higher vocationally qualified or lower qualified women.

- Childcare was seen as the primary responsibility of women regardless of the level or type of qualification held by the woman. However, highly qualified women who were in employment were more likely to say they shared childcare with their spouse/partner than women who were not in paid employment. Where highly qualified women were not in paid employment, responsibility for childcare reverted to them to a large extent.

- Domestic tasks and household chores were more likely to be shared with spouse/partner in the case of highly qualified women who were in employment. As with childcare responsibilities employment status rather than the level of qualifications held by the woman was the main element affecting who did various tasks in the household.

Introduction

This report provides information on the employment characteristics of women who have qualifications above 'A' level General Certificate of Education[1]. The employment situation, pay, employment history, attitudes to work and domestic situation of these women is examined and compared with a) highly qualified men and b) women with less or no qualifications.

Although there is now a substantial body of literature addressing the issues surrounding the position of women in the labour market, there is relatively little written about the relationship between the level and type of qualification that women hold and their consequential employment. Sources exist which provide basic statistics on the relative occupational position of women and men with and without formal educational qualifications. However, these are generally summaries and have documented little more than whether the individual holds a degree or 'A' levels. The important distinction between holding vocational and non-vocational qualifications has not been examined, other than separating out vocational qualifications such as teaching and nursing.

The analysis for this report has been carried out by the ESRC Research Centre on Micro-social Change based at the University of Essex on behalf of the Employment Department. The data are drawn from Wave 1 of the British Household Panel Study (BHPS), a national household panel survey of over 10,000 individuals in some 5,500 households in Britain. The sample was drawn from the small users file of the Postcode Address File and covers non-institutional residences in England, Wales and Scotland (north of the Caledonian Canal excluded). The BHPS is an annual survey which commenced in September 1991 and will return to re-interview panel members on an annual basis over the coming years. The BHPS questionnaires consist of the Household Composition Form which enumerates all current members of the household; the Household Questionnaire which collects information on housing tenure and costs, consumption items and household expenditure on fuel and food; the Individual Questionnaire which is administered to all adult members of the household aged 16 years and over, and collects a wide range of information including detailed employment and income information and a Self Completion Questionnaire containing attitudinal items and measures of well-being and social support.

At Wave 1 of the survey 13,840 individuals were enumerated in 5,511 households. Of these 9912 eligible adults were interviewed and 352 proxy interviews taken giving an upper response rate (full interviews with at least one member of the household) of 74%. For the purposes of the analysis reported here the sample consists of the 9,912 respondents who answered a full individual questionnaire.[2]

The BHPS collects information about education and qualifications for individuals to a level of detail comparable with the General Household Survey (GHS 1987). This covers school, further and higher educational qualifications, and specifies the type and number of each type of qualification gained by respondents in their lifetimes (see Appendix A). The BHPS dataset also provides valuable information on the domestic and household circumstances of women which may be important factors in determining a woman's decision to enter into paid employment outside the household. The BHPS will, naturally, supply unique prospective longitudinal information on the employment patterns of women over the course of the panel study. At Wave 2, a retrospective employment status history was collected providing a 'skeleton' history of transitions in and out of various states of employment. This retrospective historical information together with the data collected at Wave 1 and Wave 2 will form the basis of Phase 2 of the Highly Qualified Women Report to be completed in Spring 1994. This report primarily uses the cross-sectional information collected at Wave 1 of the BHPS to look at the current employment position of highly qualified women, although information on women's employment in the year preceding interview is also utilised.

Women in the labour market

It is well documented that women suffer discrimination in the labour market compared to their male counterparts. In most Western countries there is a clear segregation by gender within the labour market, or dual labour market, with defined primary and secondary sectors (Barron and Norris 1976). Fewer women are in professional occupations or are employers or managers whilst more are in junior non-manual and lower level manual work. Thus on average, women receive lower wages than men, occupy a smaller range of occupations, have less autonomy and responsibility in their jobs, have less security and fewer opportunities for career advancement. Putting together the time spent doing paid and unpaid work, women also spend longer hours working than men.

Since the 1980's, Britain and Europe have seen efforts made to attract women into the more male dominated educational courses or occupations. Policy drives towards a greater equality in education and employment opportunities brought with it specific initiatives such as Women in Science and Engineering, Women in Industry as well as many courses designed to help retrain women who had taken time out of the labour market to look after children.

Efforts made to draw women into the professions, such as those in the fields of science and engineering, and corporate management and administration, appear to have been successful. British statistics suggest that over the period 1970-1990 the professions showed a faster employment growth than any other sector (from 6.4% to 9.6% of total employment), and that female employment in these professional occupations grew more strongly than males (IER 1992). However, despite this unprecedented rise in the number of women entering into higher level professional occupation such as medicine, accountancy, law and pharmacy, many women are side-tracked into 'occupational niches' rather than remaining in central positions within the profession (Crompton and Sanderson 1990). In the associate professions, a gender split is still very defined with little change since the early eighties with the majority of science and engineering associate professionals being men and the majority of health associate professionals being women (IER 1992).

In additional to a boom in the professional occupations, the last decade has also seen a growth of the number of women entering management related jobs. The growth of these employment opportunities for women in this sector may be attributed to structural changes which have favoured the growth of sectors in which managerial women are traditionally found. Also there have been some positive initiatives by large companies and the Civil Service to boost the number of women in higher status posts, (IER 1992). However, women in management are most likely to be in occupations which have been traditionally female dominated such as catering and retail (Novarra 1980).

In the future it is predicted that the number of corporate managers and administrators will rise together with improved openings for women and an increased importance of achieving highly educated employees. Moreover, with the opening of the free European Market in 1992 we would expect to see a move towards pushing British employers to comply with European Community equal opportunities policies in their treatment of women employees.

Educational qualifications and success in the labour market

Educational attainment is recognised to be related to a greater participation in the labour market for women and to a stronger career position. Crompton and Sanderson (1990) suggest that many of the qualifications gained by women are gender related, for the very reason that women tend to anticipate gender segregation of subsequent employment. Thus part of the gender inequality in the labour market may be traced back to the earlier educational experience of women. The distribution of male and female students in subjects at secondary school and tertiary college is often very uneven with some subjects, such as science, being almost exclusively pursued by males, and other ones, though fewer, by females (Dolton and Makepeace 1992). Although a higher proportion of girls take one or two year vocational courses at Further Education Colleges, boys are still more likely to go to university (Skills and Enterprise Network, 1993).

Despite the increase in the number of women pursuing post-compulsory educational courses and gaining qualifications over the last few decades, women still make up the greatest proportion training to enter the teaching, nursing, midwife and pre-school occupations, and at university or polytechnic level, a gender imbalance is evident. Engineering is still a male preserve whilst women tend to specialise in arts and languages. For example, data from the 1987 graduates survey reported a fifth of male graduates studying engineering and technology at university compared to only 2% of women. Conversely, a quarter of women graduates studied language, literature and area studies compared to only 7% of men (Dolton and Makepeace ibid).

Career opportunities available to men and women who have pursued higher education are also unequal. Occupational success is commonly recognised as achieving an occupation of high standing or achieving higher earning levels, although the two may not necessarily be inter-related. Not only are many of the higher status occupations male dominated, despite the introduction of sex discrimination and equal pay legislation, but a woman's career progression in these jobs is hindered or even blocked compared to their male counterparts. This is in part a reflection of a woman's life course, where labour market participation is seen to fall after the birth of a first child followed by a return to part-time employment and later possible re-entry into full-time employment (Dex 1985; Dale and Glover 1990).

Information from the Labour Force Survey suggested that in 1989, 14% of women in Britain who were unemployed and economically inactive were educated to above 'A' level standard (Dex 1992). Figures from the 1987 follow-up of the 1980 Survey of Graduates undertaken jointly by the Employment Department and Department of Education and Science tell a similar story (Dolton and Makepeace 1992). By 1987, of those graduating in 1980, the majority of men were in employment, whilst 11% of women were economically inactive, and not seeking work, mainly due to family commitments.

The careers of highly educated women therefore suffer compared to those of men; periods spent out of the labour market by women mean that many cannot advance as far in their chosen profession as they would like, and they may have been restricted to taking part-time jobs, often of lower status, while they are raising children. The first wave of BHPS data asks about family commitments and reasons for not working, thus enabling us to focus on the groups of highly educated women and to compare their position today, at the beginning of the 1990s.

If we look further at the types of occupations into which young men and women enter into shortly after gaining their qualifications, we see large gender differences. Of graduates under the age of 30, men are most likely to be employed in industry, commerce and self-regulating professions, such as accountancy and law, whilst female graduates are most likely to enter teaching professions (Dolton and Makepeace 1992). Moreover, the 1987 data suggested that after six years out of higher education, the men in their sample had fewer job changes than the women, although the degree of mobility was highly variable in different occupational sectors. Family commitments were found to be a major influence in reasons for leaving jobs over time in the work histories of women.

Women's earnings are usually lower than men's earnings regardless of level of education or degree of training. Statistics show that seven years after graduating, men with degrees earned on average 25% more than women with equivalent qualifications (Dolton and Makepeace 1992). In addition to the gender imbalance found for earnings and status of the highly educated, previous findings also suggest that large numbers of women were working in occupations below their capacity because of downward occupational mobility. Drawing on data from the 1980 Women in Employment Survey (WES) and the 1986 Social Change and Economic Life Initiative (SCELI) Dex estimated that in 1989 between 2.9 and 3.7 million employed women were currently in occupations which under-utilised their ability, and of these women as many as a third had above 'A' level qualifications.

It is beyond the scope of this report to address the questions as to why we observe disparities in both education and occupation between the sexes. Undoubtedly a number of factors play a part; for example the educational system's methods and practices, careers counselling for children, and normative expectations for women dating back to their earlier years inside and outside the classroom. Studies show that teachers spend more time on average attending to boys than girls and that boys spend far more time in discussion in the classroom than do girls. Successfully getting a job in later life involves confidence and self-presentation skills which may reflect past activities and performance in the classroom. Furthermore, women have until recently been dissuaded from establishing themselves in the more 'masculine' subjects , such as maths and science. Some social psychological research suggests that women may tend to avoid success, and adopt a less competitive stance when choosing their career because they consider it to be unfeminine. Consequently they may avoid situations that require competition to achieve. However, educational reforms and equal opportunities policies have helped to reduce the stigma attached to becoming a `career woman'.

This analysis goes some way towards assessing the impact of the level and type of qualifications women hold on their labour market position.

Footnotes to Introduction

1. Refer to Section 1 for a full definition of 'highly qualified' women.

2. Information collected by the proxy questionnaire does not adequately cover qualifications or characteristics of employment, and proxies have been excluded from this analysis.

Section 1

Distribution of higher qualifications in the BHPS

Defining the highly qualified

This section discusses how the highly qualified have been defined for the purposes of this report and presents distributions of the BHPS sample according to their level of qualification. 'Highly qualified' is defined as holding one or more of the following classes of recognised educational qualification;

1. University or CNAA Higher Degree of UK standard;

2. University or CNAA First Degrees and all other qualifications of UK First Degree standard, including university diploma;

3. Teaching qualification (excluding degrees, classified as 1 above);

4. Nursing qualification (including SEN, SRN, SCM);

5. Higher National Certificate (HNC) or Higher National Diploma (HND), Higher BEC, TEC, BTEC Higher Certificate or Higher Diploma, City and Guilds Certificate Full Technological, Part III;

6. Other technical, professional or higher qualification considered to be at a level higher than 'A' level where any of the above qualifications are **not** held.

We have considered all the qualifications listed above to be higher than 'A' level standard, with a couple of exceptions. The coding scheme for qualifications in the Wave 1 BHPS questionnaire (given in Appendix A) does not allow us to distinguish between levels of nursing training (for example, SEN and SRN), therefore this group may contain individuals with a lower level of qualification than other groups. The classes of qualifications listed above are ranked according to the level of qualification, with (1) being considered the highest. Group (6) covers a wide range of qualifications ranging from a diploma in radiography to membership of professional institutions, or chartered accountant status. Generally, these qualifications relate to further specific training related to the individual's profession or job and therefore the group is fairly heterogenous. It should be made clear that of our highly qualified sample, any member may hold more than one of the above types of qualifications; in

this case, they will be classified according to the highest qualification they hold. That is, an individual holding a degree and a professional qualification, will be classified as having a degree, and even if their professional qualification is one of high status, such as bar exams, their grouping will not indicate this.

For the purposes of this report, 'highly qualified' refers to any respondent holding one or more of the five qualifications listed in Table 1.1a. Consequently, 'less qualified' refers to the group with either a lower level than these five qualifications or no qualifications. The term 'higher academic' is used here to denote the highly qualified group holding either a higher degree, first degree or university diplomas. Since we are specifically interested in making the distinction between vocational and non-vocational qualifications, group (1) and (2) qualifications above are considered as non-vocational, or academic, we refer to additional vocations qualifications as AVQ and the remaining groups (3) to (6) are classed as vocational.

Highest educational qualification

Tables 1.1a, 1.1b and 1.1c show the distribution of the sample's highest educational qualification by gender and age.[1] Approximately one-quarter of the sample of working age (n=1,709) held a higher qualification, of whom 44% (n=747) had a university level qualification, 22% (n=373) had teaching or nursing qualifications, and a further 23% (n=392) had an advanced BEC/BTEC/City and Guilds or equivalent qualification[2]. Men were marginally more likely to hold degree level qualifications than women, whilst a far greater proportion of men held higher BTEC or City and Guilds equivalent qualifications than women (9% compared to 2% of women). Women, on the other hand, were almost ten times more likely to hold nursing qualifications than men, and twice as many women had non-degree level teaching qualifications. Table 1.1b shows a significant difference for age in educational achievement, with over a quarter (n=1,223) of those under the age of 44 holding higher qualifications compared to only a fifth (n=483) over age 44. Almost half the number of BHPS respondents of working age over 45 held a degree or a higher BTEC or City and Guilds or equivalent than did their younger counterparts, whilst fewer in the 20-34 age group held teaching qualifications. Table 1.1c shows that men of all ages were more likely to hold degrees or equivalent than women.

Table 1.1a   BHPS 1991: Highest educational qualification by gender[a]

Women aged 20-59 and men aged 20-64

Highest educational qualification*	Women	Men	All BHPS	
	%	%	Freq	%
Higher/first degree/university diploma	9.1	11.7	749	10.4
Teaching qualification	3.1	1.2	152	2.1
Nursing qualification	5.6	.6	220	3.1
Higher BTEC/City & Guilds equivalent	1.9	8.9	392	5.5
Other higher vocational qualifications	1.6	3.7	194	2.7
None of the above	78.6	73.9	5472	76.2
Base = 100%	3503	3676	7179	

a   *Column percentage calculated on the base figures shown.*

*   *Sig <.000.*

Table 1.1b   BHPS 1991: Highest educational qualification by age[a]

Women aged 20-59 and men aged 20-64

Highest educational qualification*	20-34	35-44	45+	All BHPS	
	%	%	%	Freq	%
Higher/First degree/University diploma	12.2	12.0	7.1	749	10.4
Teaching qualification	1.0	3.0	2.8	152	2.1
Nursing qualification	3.4	2.4	3.2	220	3.1
Higher BTEC/City & Guilds equivalent	6.5	6.0	3.9	392	5.5
Other higher vocational qualifications	2.3	3.0	3.0	194	2.7
None of the above	74.7	73.6	80.1	5472	76.2
Base = 100%	2931	1822	2426	7179	

a   *Column percentage calculated on the base figures shown.*

*   *Sig. <.000.*

Table 1.1c   BHPS 1991: Highest educational qualification by gender and age[a]

Women aged 20-59 and men aged 20-64

Highest educational qualification	20-34*	35-44*	45+*	All BHPS	
	%	%	%	Freq	%
Women					
Higher/first degree/university diploma	11.1	9.7	5.9	319	9.1
Teaching qualification	1.5	4.7	4.0	109	3.1
Nursing qualification	5.9	4.5	6.1	196	5.6
Higher BTEC/City & Guilds equivalent	3.1	1.5	(.6)	67	1.9
Other higher vocational qualifications	1.8	1.5	1.5	56	1.6
None of the above	76.6	78.0	82.0	2753	78.6
Base = 100%	1483	929	1091	3503	
Men					
Higher/first degree/university diploma	13.2	14.5	8.1	430	11.7
Teaching qualification	(.5)	1.3	1.8	44	1.2
Nursing qualification	.8	(.1)	.8	22	.6
Higher BTEC/City & Guilds equivalent	10.0	10.5	6.6	327	8.9
Other higher vocational qualifications	2.7	4.6	4.2	136	3.7
None of the above	72.8	69.0	78.5	2717	73.9
Base = 100%	1448	893	1335	3676	

a   Column percentage calculated on the base figures shown.

*   Sig. <.000 (men vs women).

A cross classification of qualification by whether respondents held an additional vocational qualification (shown in Table 1.2) suggests that only 2% of the degree or teaching qualified groups held an additional vocational qualification compared to around 7% of the higher BTEC/City and Guilds equivalent group. This largely reflects the type of occupational trajectories pursued by those with vocational qualifications, who as noted earlier, are more likely to obtain 'chartered' status and affiliations to established professional institutes. Although this report is primarily concerned with individuals educated to above 'A' level standard, our definition of 'the highly qualified' does not imply that having 'A' levels is a prerequisite. Our group includes individuals who have taken alternative routes to higher or further education, such as through access courses or pursuing further or higher education courses as mature students. Table 1.3 gives the number of 'highly qualified' and 'less qualified' individuals. Of our highly qualified sample, 44% (n=332) of women and 51% (n=486) of men held one or more 'A' levels. A significantly higher proportion held 'O'levels, 80% (n=597) of women and 71% (n=680) of men, but still about a quarter of our 'highly qualified' sample did not have these basic academic qualifications. The table also shows that only 8% (n=430) of men and women without higher qualifications were educated to 'A' level, and approximately 30% (n=1,686) had 'O' levels.

Table 1.4 shows the ages of our sample of highly qualified women and men. Almost half of all the graduates in the sample were under the age of 35, with women tending to be younger than similarly qualified men. Age differences between men and women for the group with higher vocational qualifications are less pronounced, but women with vocational qualifications were younger than men in this group.

Table 1.2 BHPS 1991: Proportion of highly qualified sample holding additional vocational qualifications (AVQ) by gender[a]

Women aged 20-59 and men aged 20-64

Qualification	University degree	Teaching qualification	Nursing qualification	BTEC/ City & Guilds	Other higher VQ	All	
	%	%	%	%	%	Freq	%
Women							
With AVQ	(1.6)	(1.8)	(.6)	6.3	100.0	679	90.7
Without AVQ	98.4	98.2	99.4	93.7	-	70	9.3
Base = 100%	319	109	197	66	58	749	
*Men**							
With AVQ[b]	2.4	(1.8)	(4.5)	6.8	100.0	788	82.2
Without AVQ	97.6	98.2	95.5	93.2	-	171	17.8
Base = 100%	430	43	23	326	136	958	
All BHPS							
With AVQ	2.1	(1.8)	(1.0)	6.7	100.0	1467	85.9
Without AVQ	97.9	98.2	(99.0)	93.3	-	240	14.1
Base = 100%	749	152	220	392	194	1701	

a Column percentage calculated on the base figures shown.

b AVQ = additional vocational qualification.

Brackets denote cell sizes less than 10 cases.

* Sig <.000.

Table 1.3 BHPS 1991: Proportion holding 'A' levels and 'O' levels by highest educational qualification and gender[a]

Women aged 20-59 and men aged 20-64

Educational status	Highly qualified[b]	Less qualified[c]	All BHPS	
	%	%	Freq	%
Women				
With 'A' levels	44.4	7.5	2881	17.8
Without 'A' levels	55.6	92.5	622	82.2
With 'O' levels	79.8	33.3	1514	43.2
Without 'O' levels	20.2	66.7	1989	56.8
Base = 100%	748	2754	3503	
Men				
With 'A' levels	50.7	8.2	709	19.3
Without 'A' levels	49.3	91.8	2967	80.7
With 'O' levels	70.9	28.3	1449	39.4
Without 'O' levels	29.1	71.7	2227	60.0
Base = 100%	959	2718	3676	

a   Column percentage calculated on the base figures shown.

b   'Highly qualified' includes those with one or more of the following qualifications;

   higher degree; first degree; teaching qualification (non-degree);

   nursing qualification (any level);

   higher level BTEC/ City & Guilds or equivalent;

   other higher vocational qualifications.

c   'Less qualified' includes those without any of the above 'higher qualifications'.

Sig (men vs women ('A' levels)) = ns.

Sig (men vs women ('O' levels)) <.001.

Table 1.4 BHPS 1991: Age of the highly qualified by gender[a]

Women aged 20-59 and men aged 20-64

Age groups	Higher academic*		Higher VQ*		All highly qualified	
	Women	Men	Women	Men		
	%	%	%	%	Freq	%
20-34	51.7	44.6	42.5	38.4	742	43.5
35-44	28.2	30.1	26.6	27.9	481	28.2
45+	20.2	25.3	30.0	33.8	484	28.3
Base = 100%	319	430	430	529	1707	

a   Column percentage calculated on the base figures shown.

VQ stands for vocationally qualified

*   Sig = ns.

8

Footnotes to Section 1

1. For the purposes of comparing the occupational achievement of highly qualified women with men, the sample is restricted to those of working age; women between the ages of 20 and 59 and men from 20-64. Since the peak in women's earnings occurs at around the age of 44, the age categories; 20-34; 34-44 and 45-59 are considered.

2. Hereafter this group of vocational qualifications are referred to as higher BTEC or City and Guilds equivalent.

Section 2

Labour market position of highly qualified women

In this section we briefly examine the labour market position of highly qualified women and compare them with other women of working age. Occupational details are more fully addressed in the following sections.

Employment status

Table 2.1 gives the distribution of current employment status for women by level of education. Since marital status plays an important role in determining participation in the labour market, employment status is considered separately for the married[1] and the non-married. Of all married women in the BHPS, 30% (n=691) were not in paid employment, and of the two-thirds in paid employment (n=1,620), roughly equal numbers worked in full-time and part-time jobs. An equal proportion of non-married women were economically inactive (31% n=373) but only 49% (n=183) of these economically inactive women were looking after the home, compared to 85% (n=585) of their married counterparts. Almost three times as many of the non-married were in 'other' employment states, including full-time education, long-term sick or retired. A significantly greater proportion of non-married women worked full-time than did married women (52% compared with 30% respectively)[2].

Looking at the numbers of women with higher qualifications by marital status we see that of the 2,311 married women in the sample, 8% (n=179) had higher academic qualifications, 12% (n=286) had higher vocational qualifications and the remaining 80% (n=1,846) had less or no qualifications. This group of highly qualified married women were substantially more likely to be in paid employment than less qualified married women. Over a quarter (n=519) of the less qualified group were looking after the home compared to only 1 in 7 (n=67) of highly qualified women, whilst under two-thirds (n=1,574) of less qualified married women were in paid employment compared to 80% (n=785) of the highly qualified group. Married women with higher academic qualifications were more likely to have a full-time job or be self-employed than those with higher vocational qualifications, but less likely to have a part-time job or be unemployed[3].

When we consider non-married women of working age, we see that over 70% (n=205) of the highly qualified held a full-time job compared to 46% (n=413) of less qualified women. Only 8% (n=24) of non-married highly qualified women were in part-time jobs compared to 14% (n=125) of the less qualified. The proportions of non-married women looking after the home differ greatly by level of qualification. Six times as many non-married less qualified women than highly qualified women in the sample were looking after the home, whilst the latter group were also less likely to be unemployed than the less qualified. Finally , it is apparent that self-employment is positively associated with level of qualification, with 10% (n=14) of non-married women graduates being self-employed compared to 5% (n=7) of the vocationally qualified group and even fewer, under 3% (n=25) of the less qualified.

Table 2.2 suggests that highly qualified women with academic qualifications were almost twice as likely to be self-employed than vocationally qualified women or women with less qualifications.

Usual hours of work

Tables 2.3a and 2.3b set out the distribution of working hours for women in employment by marital status and presence of dependent children. Seventeen percent (n=25) of higher academic married women worked a 40 plus hour week compared to only 11% of married women with higher vocational qualifications or less qualifications. As discussed earlier, vocationally qualified married women are more likely to work part-time, and Table 2.3a shows that almost twice as many of our vocationally qualified women worked under 16 hours per week than their academically qualified counterparts. For the non-married in paid employment, significantly more higher academic women, 34% (n=41) worked a 40 or more hour week compared to only 16% (n=21) of the vocationally qualified, whilst the majority, 71% (n=91) of non-married women with higher vocational qualifications worked 30-39 hours per week in their jobs. Sixteen or less hour week jobs were almost non-existant for non-married academically qualified women.

From Table 2.3b it can be seen that having dependent children is associated with working hours. The proportion working over 40 hours a week are similar for both groups of highly qualified

Table 2.1   BHPS 1991: Employment status of women by level of qualification and marital status[a]

Married women aged 20-59

Employment status*	Higher academic %	Higher VQ %	Less qualified %	All women Freq	All women %
Full-time paid employment	51.2	40.8	26.4	696	30.1
Part-time paid employment[b]	23.2	28.7	33.4	741	32.1
Self-employed	9.2	5.7	5.6	135	5.9
Unemployed	(1.0)	2.1	2.1	46	2.0
Looking after the home	12.4	15.6	28.1	586	25.3
Other[c]	(3.0)	7.1	4.4	106	2.6
Base = 100%	179	286	1846	2311	

*   *Sig <.000.*

Non-married women aged 20-59

Employment status*	Higher academic %	Higher VQ %	Less qualified %	All women Freq	All women %
Full-time paid employment	70.2	74.5	45.9	620	52.2
Part-time paid employment[b]	8.0	8.9	13.8	149	12.5
Self-employed	10.0	(5.1)	2.8	47	3.9
Unemployed	(3.5)	(3.0)	8.2	84	7.1
Looking after the home	1.8	3.6	19.3	183	15.4
Other[c]	6.5	4.8	9.9	105	8.9
Base = 100%	140	143	905	1187	

VQ refers to vocational qualifications

a   *Column percentage calculated on the base figures shown.*

b   *Part-time employment is defined as working 30 hours or less per week.*

c   *Other category includes those in full-time education, long-term sick, retired and others.*

Brackets denote cell sizes less than 10 cases.

*   *Sig <.000.*

Table 2.2   BHPS 1991: Employee status of all women in paid employment by level of qualification[a]

Women aged 20-59

Employment status*	Higher academic %	Higher VQ %	Less qualified %	All women Freq	All women %
Employee	88.5	93.2	92.6	2225	92.2
Self-employed	11.5	6.8	7.4	188	7.8
Base = 100%	273	343	1796	2413	

a   *Column percentage calculated on the base figures shown.*

*   *Sig < .05.*

11

Table 2.3a   BHPS 1991: Usual working hours per week in paid employment by level of qualification and marital status[a]

Married women aged 20-59 in employment

Employment status*	Higher academic	Higher VQ	Less qualified	All women	
	%	%	%	Freq	%
*Hours worked per week**					
< 16 hours	11.5	19.3	21.8	316	20.5
16-29 hours	19.4	21.9	31.6	449	29.1
30-39 hours	51.8	47.6	35.2	593	38.4
40+ hours	17.3	11.2	11.5	186	12.0
Base = 100%	146	209	118	1544	

Non-married women aged 20-59 in employment

Employment status*	Higher academic	Higher VQ	Less qualified	All women	
	%	%	%	Freq	%
*Hours worked per week**					
< 16 hours	(1.5)	(5.5)	9.0	60	7.4
16-29 hours	8.0	(6.8)	14.7	102	12.5
30-39 hours	56.4	71.4	57.4	486	59.4
40+ hours	34.0	16.4	18.9	170	20.8
Base = 100%	121	127	571	819	

VQ refers to vocational qualifications

a   Column percentage calculated on the base figures shown.

Brackets denote cell sizes less than 10 cases.

*   Sig < .000.*

women with pre-school age children and school age children. However, over half of higher academic mothers of school age children worked a 30-39 hour week compared to 38% (n=33) of the vocationally qualified.

Occupations

Table 2.4 shows the distribution of occupations for highly qualified women in employment. The Standard Occupational Classification (SOC 1990) is used to classify occupations. Minor Groups in SOC are distinguished by reference to the type of work performed or the area of occupational specialism which characterises the constituent unit groups. The Minor Groups are aggregated into 22 Sub-major Groups which distinguish between the broader

groups of occupations. The Sub-major Groups are further classified together into nine SOC Major Groups (shown in Appendix B) on the basis of the qualifications, training or work experience associated with the 'competent performance of work tasks' (p. 4, SOC Vol 1, 1990). For the highest six groups the following distinctions between occupations are important; Major Group 1 which includes managers and administrators identifies two distinct groups, separating out managers of small business and other managers; in Major Group 2 for professional occupations, four groups are classified distinguishing between science and engineering, health, education, and other professionals; in a similar way, Major Group 3 contains 3 distinct groups of science and engineering, health and other associate professionals; for Group 4 clerical and secretarial occupations are classified separately

Table 2.3b   BHPS 1991: Usual working hours per week in paid employment by level of qualification and presence of dependent children[a]

Married women aged 20-59 in employment

Employment status*	Higher academic	Higher VQ	Less qualified	All women	
	%	%	%	Freq	%
*Hours worked per week**					
No dependent children					
<16 hours	(3.1)	7.2	9.6	121	8.4
16-29 hours	9.6	9.3	20.1	246	17.1
30-39 hours	56.1	69.2	53.0	802	55.8
40+ hours	31.2	14.3	17.3	268	18.7
Base = 100%	186	212	1039		1437
Children aged less than 5					
<16 hours	28.4	(21.0)	26.9	48	25.9
16-29 hours	34.0	30.8	34.6	62	33.8
30-39 hours	23.5	31.6	28.5	53	28.6
40+ hours	14.1	(16.6)	9.9	21	11.7
Base = 100%	20	35	129		184
Children 5-15					
<16 hours	(11.5)	28.4	29.7	209	28.1
16-29 hours	21.3	26.1	34.8	244	32.8
30-39 hours	57.4	37.5	26.7	225	30.2
40+ hours	9.8	(9.1)	8.7	66	8.9
Base = 100%	61	88	595	744	

VQ refers to vocational qualifications

a   Column percentage calculated on the base figures shown.

Brackets denote cell sizes less than 10 cases.

*   Sig < .000.

whilst for Major Group 5 the skilled occupations distinguish between construction, engineering and other trades. Sub-major Group 6 classifies protective and personal services separately. In Table 2.4 both the Major SOC and Sub-major Group are shown, although in the case of the lowest five groups, the Sub-major Groups do not contain enough cases of women to justify reporting.[4]

Academically qualified women were most likely to be in the top three major occupational groups compared to vocationally qualified women or women with less qualifications (83%, 64% and 14% respectively). Highly qualified women were also less likely to be in clerical or secretarial occupations than less qualified women, whilst even fewer of the highly qualified occupied the lower SOC groups, with the exception of 12% of vocationally qualified women who worked in personal services.

Of the highly qualified women, just under half (n=128) of the academically qualified held jobs in professional occupations whilst comparatively fewer women (19%; n=65) with vocational qualifications held these higher status professional jobs, but they did tend to occupy the 'associate professional' occupations (38%). Thirteen percent (n=36) of the academically qualified held managerial type posts compared to 9% (n=30) of the vocationally qualified.

Table 2.4   BHPS 1991: Standard Occupational Classification (Major Group) of women in full-time, part-time paid and self-employment by level of qualification[a]

Women aged 20-59

SOC Major and Sub-major Groups	Higher academic			Higher VQ			Less qualified			All women		
	Freq	%[a]	%[b]	Freq	%[a]	%[b]	Freq	%[a]	%[b]	Freq	%[a]	%[b]
Managers and administrators	**36**	**13.3**		**30**	**8.8**		**143**	**8.0**		**209**	**8.7**	
Corporate managers and administrators			86.1			56.7			38.5			48.8
Managers/proprietors in agriculture and services			(13.9)			43.3			61.5			51.2
Professional	**128**	**47.2**		**65**	**19.1**		**30**	**1.7**		**224**	**9.3**	
Science and engineering professionals			(3.1)			(3.1)			(6.7)			(3.6)
Health professionals			(6.3)			-			(.1)			4.9
Teaching professionals			63.3			84.6			36.7			66.1
Other professionals			27.3			(12.3)			46.7			25.4
Associate professional and technical	**61**	**22.5**		**130**	**38.1**		**99**	**5.5**		**294**	**12.2**	
Science and engineering associate professionals			26.2			(3.9)			11.1			10.9
Health associate professionals			21.3			81.5			20.2			47.6
Other associate professionals			52.5			14.6			68.7			40.5
Clerical and secretarial	**28**	**10.3**		**54**	**15.8**		**615**	**34.4**		**699**	**29.0**	
Clerical occupations			75.0			63.0			69.9			69.2
Secretarial occupations			(25.0)			37.0			30.1			30.8

Brackets denote cell sizes less than 10 cases.

14

Table 2.4 BHPS 1991: Standard Occupational Classification (Major Group) of women in full-time, part-time paid and self-employment by level of qualification[a] (continued)

Women aged 20-59

SOC Major and Sub-major Groups	Higher academic		Higher VQ		Less qualified		All women	
	Freq	%[a]	Freq	%[a]	Freq	%[a]	Freq	%[a]
Craft and related occupations[c]	2	(0.7)	3	(0.9)	71	4.0	76	3.1
Personal/protective service[d]	8	(3.0)	42	12.3	285	15.9	335	13.9
Sales[e]	6	(2.2)	6	(1.8)	207	11.6	220	9.1
Plant and machine operatives[f]	2	(0.7)	6	(1.8)	96	5.4	103	4.3
Other occupations[g]	-		5	(1.5)	241	13.5	246	10.2
Base = 100%	271		341		1787		2406	

VQ refers to vocational qualifications

a   Column percentage calculated on the base figures shown in the final row.

b   Column percentage calculated on the base figures shown for each SOC Major Group (shown in bold).

c   The majority of women in these groups were in skilled trades other than construction and engineering.

d   Only a very small minority of women were in protective service occupations.

e   Very few women were buyers, brokers and sales representatives, but occupied the 'other sales' category.

f   No women in the BHPS sample were in industrial plant and machine operators and assemblers occupations.

g   Very few women in the other elementary occupations work in the field of agriculture, forestry and fishing.

Brackets denote cell sizes less than 10 cases.

When we break down these SOC Major Groups into their constituent sub groups, we find that the 86% (n=31) of the 'academic' women managers were corporate managers or administrators compared to only 57% (n=17) of their vocationally qualified counterparts. Thus we see relatively few 'academic' women in 'managers/proprietors in agriculture and services' occupations. It is also interesting to note that a far greater proportion of less qualified women in 'managerial' posts were managers or proprietors in services (62%, n=88).

In the 'professional' occupations, almost three-quarters (70%, n=136) of highly qualified women were located in the teaching professions, although 20% more vocationally qualified professionals were teachers (n=55) than their academically qualified counterparts (n=81). Very few women worked in science and engineering professional occupations. We see a more striking difference between academically and vocationally qualified women for the 'associate professional' occupations; four times as many of the vocationally qualified (81%, n=106) in this SOC group worked in the health field compared to academically qualified women (21%, n=13). Furthermore, we see a far smaller proportion of the vocationally qualified associate professionals working in science or engineering jobs than we do for academically qualified women (26% of qualified women compared to only 4% of vocationally qualified). Academically qualified women generally tended to occupy a broader range of associate professional occupations with over half (n=32) working in fields other than health or science and engineering compared to only 15% (n=19) of vocationally qualified associate professionals.

When we consider women in clerical and secretarial occupations, we see that only a quarter (n=7) of graduates in this SOC Major Group were in secretarial posts, whilst for both vocationally qualified women and less qualified women in this group, a third (n=20 and n=185 respectively) were secretaries.

The distribution of occupations for both groups of highly qualified women differs very little for women under the age of 44 and those over age 44, but shows fairly marked differences according to marital status (not shown here). Married women, typically work fewer hours in their jobs, and are therefore often in less prestigous jobs. For the group of academically qualified women, non-married women were twice as likely to be in managerial occupations as married{5} women but 12% less likely to hold professional posts than their married counterparts.[5] For those women holding vocational qualifications, 6% more married women occupied professional and associate professional jobs than non-married women.

Managerial responsibilities

Table 2.5 sets out the proportion of women in jobs with managerial or supervisory responsibilities. For highly qualified women in full-time jobs, almost twice as many with academic qualifications had managerial duties compared to vocational qualified women (40% compared to 23% respectively), whilst the reverse situation was true for supervisory responsibilities. Only one-third (n=305) of less or non-qualified women reported having some managerial or supervisory responsibility in their job at the time of interview.

Table 2.5   BHPS 1991: Managerial responsibilities of full-time employed women by level of qualification[a]

Women aged 20-59

Managerial/supervisory* responsibilities	Higher academic %	Higher VQ %	Less qualified %	All women Freq	%
Manager	39.5	22.9	13.9	251	19.1
Foreman/supervisor	17.6	36.6	19.8	294	22.4
Neither manager or supervisor	42.9	40.5	66.2	769	58.5
Base = 100%	190	222	903	1314	

a   Column percentage calculated on the base figures shown.

*   Sig < .000.

Footnotes to Section 2

1. 'Married' includes those co-habiting.

2. Full-time employment is defined as working 30 hours or more per week.

3. The unemployed are defined in accordance with the LFS (ILO/OECD) i.e. all those not currently employed who either looked for work at some time in the last four weeks or were waiting to take up a job already obtained.

4. In the BHPS sample, women in the 'craft and related occupations' were largely located in 'other skilled trades' with almost none in construction and engineering, and of the 'protective and personal' Major Group only a very small minority of women were in protective service occupations. Similarly, of the 'sales' Major SOC Group, very few women were buyers, brokers and sales representatives, and of the 'Plant and machine operators' Major Group, no women in the BHPS sample were industrial plant, machine operators or assemblers. Finally, only a handful of women in the 'other elementary occupations' Major Group worked in the field of agriculture, forestry and fishing.

5. Evidence further suggests that it is not just single women who are more likely to hold managerial posts, but that the women who do are likely not to have children.

Section 3

Employment characteristics of highly qualified men and women

In this section we compare some of the basic characteristics of employment for highly qualified women and men. Section 4 looks further at utilisation of qualifications in the labour market for our highly qualified sample.

Employment status

Table 3.1 compares the current employment status of men and women of working age by level of qualification. As discussed earlier, academically qualified women are more likely to be working in full-time and less likely to be in part-time employment jobs or looking after the home than vocationally qualified women. This association between type of qualification and being in full-time employment is not evident for highly qualified men, of whom over 80% of both graduates and vocationally qualified (n=355 and n=447 respectively) were working in full-time jobs. Although comparatively few highly qualified men were in part-time jobs, a greater proportion of higher

academic men worked part-time compared to their vocationally qualified counterparts. Twice as many highly qualified men than women were unemployed, regardless of type of qualification. Both men and women with higher qualifications were twice as less likely to be unemployed than their less qualified counterparts.

Table 3.2 shows the proportion of the highly qualified men and women who are self-employed. Overall, over half as many women were self-employed as men, but this difference being less pronounced for the higher academic group. Eighteen percent of both academically and vocationally qualified men were self-employed (n=70 and n=83 respectively), whilst academic women are more likely to be self-employed than vocationally qualified women (12% compared to 7% respectively).

Usual hours of work

Table 3.3 gives the distribution of number of hours usually worked in current job for highly qualified men and women in paid employment. We noted earlier that more higher academic women than vocationally qualified women worked a 40 or more hour week. For highly qualified men, the distribution of work hours is almost identical for the two groups, of whom almost 40% worked 40 hours or more in their jobs. The proportion of men and women working a 30-39 hour week is virtually identical, with very little difference between qualification groups.

Table 3.1   BHPS 1991: Employment status of the highly qualified by gender[a]

Women aged 20-59 and men aged 20-64

Employment status	Higher academic*		Higher VQ*		Less qualified		All BHPS	
	Women	Men	Women	Men	Women	Men		
	%	%	%	%	%	%	Freq	%
In full-time employment	66.1	82.5	54.9	84.4	36.2	74.5	4269	59.5
In part-time employment	19.5	7.5	24.7	3.4	28.3	3.4	1091	15.2
Unemployed	(2.1)	4.4	2.4	4.9	4.1	10.9	471	6.6
Looking after the home	7.7	-	11.6	-	25.2	.5	783	10.9
Other[b]	4.6	5.6	6.4	7.2	6.2	10.7	556	7.9
Base = 100%	319	430	430	529	2754	2718	7170	

a   Column percentage calculated on the base figures shown.

b   Other category includes those in full-time education, long-term sick, retired and others.

*   Sig <.000.

Brackets denote cell sizes less than 10 cases.

18

Table 3.2   BHPS 1991: Employee status for highly qualified men and women in paid employment[a]

Women aged 20-59 and men aged 20-64

Employment status	Higher academic*		Higher VQ*		All employed**			
	Women	Men	Women	Men	Women	Men	All	
	%	%	%	%	%	%	Freq	%
Employee	88.4	82.0	97.2	82.0	92.0	81.3	4660	86.3
Self-employee	11.6	18.0	6.9	17.8	7.7	16.6	738	13.7
Base = 100%	273	387	342	464	2392	2960	5398	

a   Column percentage calculated on the base figures shown.

8 cases with missing information are excluded.

*   *Sig < .05.*

** *Sig < .000 (Men vs Women).*

Brackets denote cell sizes less than 10 cases.

Table 3.3   BHPS 1991: Usual working hours per week for the highly qualified in paid employment by gender[a]

Women aged 20-59 and men aged 20-64

Usual hours of work per week	Higher academic*		Higher VQ*		All employed**			
	Women	Men	Women	Men	Women	Men	All	
	%	%	%	%	%	%	Freq	%
< 16 hours	6.7	(1.2)	13.7	(1.0)	15.9	1.7	428	8.1
16-29 hours	14.3	3.5	16.0	(2.1)	25.3	2.1	615	11.6
30-39 hours	54.1	56.0	57.0	57.1	46.2	48.6	2496	47.1
40+ hours	25.0	39.3	13.3	39.9	15.0	47.9	1763	33.3
Base = 100%	272	366	333	257	2341	2900	5302	

a   Column percentage calculated on the base figures shown.

119 cases with missing information are excluded.

*   *Sig <.000.*

** *Sig <.000 (Men vs Women).*

Brackets denote cell sizes less than 10 cases.

Occupations

Table 3.4 suggests that similar proportions (almost 3 out of 4) of highly qualified men and women were in the top three occupations groups constituting managers, professionals and associate professionals. Although we do detect a greater gender balance for our highly qualified sample in many of the occupational groups, the lower status occupations, remain to be gender dominated following the patterns we observe in the general population. Thirteen percent (n=82) of highly qualified women fall into the clerical/secretarial group compared to only 6% (n=51) of men, whilst 12% (n=100) of highly qualified men were currently in skilled craft jobs compared to a tiny minority of women (under 1%, n=5). The gender difference for the less qualified group in the skilled craft occupations is less than for the highly qualified (29% of men compared to 4% of women).

19

Occupational status, promotion prospects and earnings are associated with full-time or part-time employment status. Table 3.5 shows the occupational distribution for the full and part-time working highly qualified groups. There is a positive relationship between occupational status and the tendency to work full time. For example, women in managerial and administrative jobs largely work full-time (89%, n=56), whereas as we descend the occupation hierarchy, we find about three-quarters of women (n=279) in the professions and associate professions in full-time positions, and even fewer (60%, n=29) in personal services working full-time.

The type of higher qualification is clearly associated with occupational status. Entry into many of the higher status jobs, such as the professions, requires a degree, whilst other types of occupations require specific vocational qualifications, such as teaching or nursing. Table 3.6 gives a further breakdown of current occupational position of our highly qualified sample according to the type of qualification they have. We see an immediate difference in occupancy of the higher status jobs according to type of

qualification. Over 83% of higher academic men (n=322) and women (n=226) were in the highest three SOC Major Groups compared to only two-thirds of vocationally trained men and women (n=287 and n= 225 respectively). The professional class show the most pronounced difference for the two qualified groups, with nearly one-half of the higher academic group having professional jobs compared to under a fifth of the vocationally qualified.

For the majority of SOC Major Groups, we find gender differences are decidedly more marked for the vocationally trained. Roughly equal proportions of higher academic men and women occupied the professional and associate professional classes. For the vocationally trained associate professionals were twice as likely to be women (38%, n=129) than men (20%, n=91). Graduate women did not appear to be as disadvantaged, compared to men, as their vocationally qualified counterparts in entering managerial or administrative jobs. Of graduates, 18% (n=69) of men and 13% (n=36) of women were in the top SOC Major Group, compared to 23%

Table 3.4   BHPS 1991: Standard Occupational Classification (Major Group) of highly qualified men and women in paid employment[ab]

Women aged 20-59 and men aged 20-64

Major SOC*	Highly qualified women %	Highly qualified men %	All employed Freq	%
Managers and professional occupations	73.6	72.4	1828	33.9
Clerical and secretarial occupations	13.4	5.9	935	17.3
Craft occupations	(.8)	11.7	792	14.7
Personal and sales occupations	10.2	6.1	844	15.6
Plant and other occupations	2.0	3.9	1000	18.5
Base = 100%	614	858	5398	

a   Column percentage calculated on the base figures shown.

b   The collapsed SOC groups are as follows;

   Managers and professional - Managers and Administrators, Professional Occupations,

   Associate Professional and Technical Occupations;

   Clerical and secretarial - Clerical and Secretarial Occupations;

   Craft occupations - Craft and Related Occupations;

   Personal and sales - Personal and Protective Service Occupations, Sales Occupations;

   Plant and other - Plant and Machine Operatives; Other Occupations.

29 cases with missing information excluded.

Brackets denote cell sizes less than 10 cases.

*   *Sig <.000.*

Table 3.5   BHPS 1991: Standard Occupational Classification (Major Group) by full-time or part-time status by gender[a]

Women aged 20-59 and men aged 20-64

SOC Major Groups	Employed women				Employed men			
	Full-time row %	Part-time row %	All Freq	col.%	Full-time row %	Part-time row %	All Freq	col.%
Highly qualified								
Managers and Administrators	88.8	11.2	63	10.6	97.8	(2.2)	169	20.6
Professional Occupations	75.9	24.1	187	31.3	95.3	4.7	261	31.8
Ass. Professional and Tech.Occs.	73.1	26.9	188	31.5	95.8	(4.2)	161	19.6
Clerical and Secretarial Occs.	71.1	28.9	81	13.6	97.3	(2.7)	51	6.2
Craft and Related Occs.	(60.0)	(40.0)	5	(.8)	96.1	(3.9)	99	12.0
Personal and Prot Service Occs.	60.1	39.9	49	8.2	100.0	-	18	2.2
Sales Occupations	(68.9)	(31.1)	12	2.0	93.7	(6.3)	31	3.8
Plant and Machine Operatives	(100.0)	-	8	1.3	100.0	-	24	2.9
Other Occupations	(40.0)	(60.0)	5	(8.0)	83.4	16.6	8	(1.0)
Base = 100%	443	154	597		791	31	822	
All BHPS employed								
Managers and Administrators	89.1	10.9	203	8.7	98.5	(1.5)	486	59.1
Professional Occupations	74.7	25.3	217	9.3	94.4	5.6	311	37.8
Ass. Professional and Tech.Occs.	74.4	25.6	283	12.1	96.4	3.6	269	32.7
Clerical and Secretarial Occs.	67.0	33.0	684	29.3	94.3	5.7	233	28.3
Craft and Related Occs.	76.8	23.2	72	3.1	97.9	2.1	703	85.5
Personal and Prot. Service Occs.	48.0	52.0	322	13.8	95.8	(4.2)	157	19.1
Sales Occupations	36.4	63.6	1213	52.0	93.1	(6.9)	116	14.1
Plant and Machine Operatives	71.0	29.0	100	4.3	98.9	(1.1)	448	54.5
Other Occupations	24.1	75.9	239	10.2	94.7	5.3	184	22.4
Base = 100%	1428	906	2334		2796	92	2888	

a   Column percentage calculated on the base figures shown in the final row.

Brackets denote cell sizes less than 10 cases.

(n=106) of men and only 9% (n=30) of women with vocational qualifications. It is interesting to note that less qualified women were no less likely to be in managerial or administrative occupations than women with higher vocational qualifications, whereas men with a higher vocational qualification had a greater chance of being in this class than men without a higher qualification, 23% (n=106) compared to 15% (n=312) respectively.

Although fewer higher academic women were in clerical or secretarial occupations than vocationally trained women, still as many as 10% (n=28) of higher academic women occupied this class, this being twice the proportion for men (n=19). Significantly fewer higher academics were employed in lower status jobs than was the case for the vocationally qualified groups, and the gender imbalance within these occupational groups was generally greater for the vocational group. For example in 'personal and professional services', we see four times as many vocationally qualified men as women in these jobs (12% compared to 4%), whereas the number of graduate men and women in these jobs is tiny.

Table 3.6   BHPS 1991: Standard Occupational Classification (Major Group) of highly qualified women and men in paid employment[a]

Women aged 20-59 and men aged 20-64

SOC Major Groups	Higher academic*		Higher VQ**		Less qualified		All BHPS	
	Women	Men	Women	Men	Women	Men		
	%	%	%	%	%	%	Freq	%
Managers and Administrators	13.2	18.1	8.7	22.7	8.0	14.6	697	12.9
Professional Occupations	47.0	47.0	18.9	19.4	1.7	2.5	553	10.2
Associate Professional and Technical Occupations	22.4	19.0	38.3	19.5	5.7	5.4	578	10.7
Clerical and Secretarial Occupations	10.2	5.1	16.0	7.1	34.4	8.7	935	17.3
Craft and Related Occupations	(0.7)	3.8	(0.9)	18.4	4.0	28.9	792	14.7
Personal and Protective Service Occupations	(3.1)	(1.5)	12.3	3.0	15.9	6.7	498	9.2
Sales Occupations	(2.3)	3.2	(1.8)	4.4	11.6	4.4	346	6.4
Plant and Machine Operatives	(0.7)	(1.0)	(1.7)	4.5	5.4	20.1	557	10.3
Other Occupations	-	(1.0)	(1.4)	(0.9)	13.4	8.8	443	8.2
Base = 100%	272	393	341	466	1792	2134	5398	

a   Column percentage calculated on the base figures shown in the final row.

Brackets denote cell sizes less than 10 cases.

*   Sig <.01.

**   Sig <.000.

A more detailed breakdown of occupations into the Sub-major Groups is given in Table 3.7. In the 'managers and administrators' occupations both higher academic men and women were largely concentrated in the corporate sector, whilst a greater proportion of the vocationally qualified were found in 'managers or proprietors in agriculture or services' occupations. The proportion of men in corporate or administrative jobs is far greater than that of women with equivalent levels of qualifications. Indeed, this sector is the dominant one for men with vocational qualifications, with almost 1 in 5 of these men being corporate managers or administrators.

Within the professions, which make up almost a half of all graduate jobs, almost two-thirds (n=81) of higher academic women professionals were teachers, compared to only a third (n=60) of their male counterparts. Highly academically qualified women were significantly under-represented in the science and engineering professions and also in the health professions; six times as many highly academically qualified men were science or engineering professionals than women. A greater number of higher academic women were in associate professional science and engineering and health occupations than men, suggesting that they are confined to these lower status jobs within these occupational fields.

When we consider the numbers of vocationally qualified men and women in the professions and associate professions, a gender inequality is once more evident. Almost 10% (n=44) of men with vocational qualifications were science and engineering professionals whereas virtually no women with the same level of qualifications held these jobs (0.5%, n=2). Women with vocational qualifications were mostly, almost 1 in 3 (n=106), situated in health associate professional jobs and after that, in the teaching professions, 17% (n=55).

The personal service occupations were also important for vocationally qualified women, of whom 12% were in these occupations (n=40), whilst very few higher academic women or men held these jobs. Sales and buying jobs were relatively unimportant for all highly qualified women, but equal numbers of men (about 3%) with either type of higher qualification were in this group.

Table 3.7   BHPS 1991: Standard Occupational Classification (Sub-major) of highly qualified men and women in paid employment[a]

Women aged 20-59 and men aged 20-64

Sub-major SOC	Higher academic*		Higher VQ*		All BHPS employees*			
	Women %	Men %	Women %	Men %	Women %	Men %	All Freq	All %
Corporate Managers and Administration	11.3	16.3	4.9	19.1	4.3	11.7	448	8.4
Managers / Proprietors in Agriculture and Services	(1.9)	(2.0)	3.3	3.7	4.5	4.8	247	4.6
Science and Engineering Professionals	(1.6)	13.2	(0.5)	9.6	(0.3)	4.1	128	2.4
Health Professionals	(2.9)	7.2	-	-	0.5	1.0	40	0.7
Teaching Professionals	30.0	15.7	16.4	3.2	6.2	2.6	226	4.2
Other Professional Occupations	13.0	11.7	(2.2)	6.8	2.4	3.4	156	2.9
Science and Engineering Associate Professionals	6.0	4.7	(1.5)	6.5	1.4	3.3	129	2.4
Health Associate Professionals	4.7	(1.0)	31.6	4.6	5.9	.9	165	3.1
Other Associate Professionals Occupations	11.7	13.3	5.7	8.7	5.0	5.3	275	5.2
Clerical Occupations	7.6	4.3	10.0	6.4	20.3	7.6	708	13.3
Secretarial Occupations	(2.6)	(0.4)	6.0	(.8)	8.9	(0.3)	221	4.2
Skilled Construction Trades	-	(0.3)	-	(1.6)	(0.1)	4.3	127	2.4
Skilled Engineering Trades	-	(2.2)	-	9.0	(0.1)	7.5	224	4.2
Other Skilled Trades	(0.7)	(1.2)	(.9)	7.6	2.9	12.2	429	8.1
Protective Service Occupations	(0.3)	(0.4)	-	2.4	(0.4)	3.1	99	1.9
Personal Service Occupations	2.7	(1.1)	11.9	(.4)	13.4	2.3	386	7.2

Continued on next page

Table 3.7 BHPS 1991: Standard Occupational Classification (Sub-major) of highly qualified men and women in paid employment[a] (continued)

Women aged 20-59 and men aged 20-64

Sub-major SOC	Higher academic*		Higher VQ*		All BHPS employees*			
	Women	Men	Women	Men	Women	Men	All	All
	%	%	%	%	%	%	Freq	%
Buyers, Brokers and Sales Representatives	(1.1)	2.6	(.3)	3.0	1.0	2.5	98	1.8
Other Sales Occupations	(1.2)	(0.4)	(1.5)	(1.3)	8.0	1.6	237	4.5
Industrial Plant and Machine Operators, Assemblers	-	-	-	-	-	-	-	-
Drivers and Mobile Machine Operators, Assemblers	(0.7)	(0.7)	(1.7)	2.4	3.9	7.9	325	6.1
Other Occupations in Agriculture, Forestry and Fishing	-	(0.6)	-	2.1	1.1	8.7	282	5.3
Other Elementary Occupations	-	(0.9)	(1.4)	(0.7)	9.5	5.1	377	7.1
Base = 100%	271	381	337	461	2378	2953	5331	

a   Column percentage calculated on the base figures shown.

Brackets denote cell sizes less than 10 cases

*   Sig = .000.

24

Industrial sector

Table 3.8 gives a breakdown of the industrial sector in which highly qualified employees are located. Over half (n=170) of higher academic males and as many as 70% (n=262) of men with vocational qualifications worked in private firms or companies. The comparative figure for women was only 30%, regardless of type of qualification. For higher academic women, local government or local education and services were the most popular sectors (42%, n=102), whilst under half the equivalent proportion of males (19%, n=59) worked in this sector. The same gender split is observed for the vocationally trained of whom 26% (n=82) of women and 13% (n=50) of men were employed in local government and related jobs. In the case of vocationally qualified women, however, a significant proportion (32%, n=100) worked for the National Health Service (mostly nursing) or in state higher education. More men worked in Civil Service or central government positions regardless of types of higher qualification.

Table 3.9 gives a breakdown of the gender mix of occupations currently held by highly qualified employees. The gender distribution for both highly qualified groups show significant differences. A fifth (n=47) of higher academic women were in jobs either mostly or exclusively done by men whilst only 9% (n=28) of the males were in jobs mostly or exclusively done by women. A significantly smaller proportion (8%) of vocationally qualified women were in male dominated jobs, and similarly only 6% (n=21) of their male counterparts were in female dominated jobs. A third of higher academic women and men worked in jobs with an equal gender mix, compared to under a quarter of vocationally trained women and men.

Table 3.8   BHPS 1991: Industry sector of current occupation for highly qualified employees by gender[a]

Women aged 20-59 and men aged 20-64 in paid employment

Industry Sector	Higher academic*		Higher VQ*		All BHPS**			
	Women	Men	Women	Men	Women	Men	All	
	%	%	%	%	%	%	Freq	%
Private firm/company/plc	30.1	53.9	32.2	69.0	59.2	74.2	3081	67.0
Civil Service/central government	6.5	9.5	(1.3)	6.5	4.1	5.6	224	4.9
Local govt./town hall/(incl. local education, fire, police)	42.3	18.8	26.0	13.1	19.5	10.1	672	14.6
National Health Service or State Higher Education	12.6	8.5	31.5	5.6	11.3	3.3	328	4.1
Other[b]	8.5	9.3	9.0	5.8	5.9	6.8	294	6.4
Base = 100%	241	315	317	379	2195	2403	4598	

a   Column percentage calculated on the base figures shown.

b   'Other' category includes nationalised industries, non-profit making organisations (e.g. charities, co-operatives).

Brackets denote cell sizes less than 10 cases.

4 cases with missing information are excluded.

*   Sig <.000.

**   Sig <.000 (Men vs Women).

Table 3.9   BHPS 1991: Gender balance of current occupation for highly qualified men and women employment (full-time and part-time)[ab]

Women aged 20-59 and men aged 20-64 in paid employment

Gender balance of current occupation	Higher academic*		Higher VQ*		All BHPS**			
	Women	Men	Women	Men	Women	Men	All	
	%	%	%	%	%	%	Freq	%
Exclusively/mostly done by men	20.4	59.2	7.6	73.3	8.2	74.9	1919	43.6
Equal mix of men and women	34.9	31.8	25.9	21.0	26.6	20.5	1029	23.3
Exclusively/mostly done by women	44.8	9.0	66.5	5.7	75.2	4.7	1462	33.2
Base = 100%	233	306	305	371	2074	2335	4409	

a   Column percentage calculated on the base figures shown.

b   Self-employed are excluded.

4 cases with missing information are excluded.

*   Sig <.000.

**   Sig <.000 (Men vs Women).*

Section 4

Utilisation of qualifications for highly qualified men and women in the labour market

Educational requirements of occupations

As mentioned in the previous section, the Major Groups in the OPCS Standard Occupational Classification (SOC) were created to provide a categorisation which brings together broadly heterogeneous occupations, on the basis of the qualifications, training or work experience associated with the competent performance of work tasks. In trying to assess utilisation of qualifications it is necessary to set up a classification which identifies occupations which demand a similar level of educational attainment or qualification. For the purposes of this report SOC provides a roughly adequate schema, given that the rationale for the Major Group classification includes qualification requirements, even if only in the broadest sense. Appendix C lists the criteria generally deemed necessary for a job to be classified in any particular Major Group.

There are, however, some problems in using the SOC Major Groups *per se* as a proxy for qualification requirements for the occupations in each group, basically because the guidance used for SOC classification is not entirely clear cut. For example, the SOC Major Group of 'managers and administrators' require 'a significant amount of knowledge and experience of the production process, administrative procedures or service requirements associated with the efficient functioning of organisations and businesses' (SOC ibid.), without specifying whether any qualifications are necessary.

Work carried out by the Institute for Economic Research (IER 1992) suggested that in 1989, of corporate managers and administrators, a quarter held a degree and a quarter held intermediate qualification, whilst of managers and proprietors in agriculture and services, only 8% held a degree and 20% intermediate qualifications. Thus these groups should be considered separately in terms of qualification requirements. It is likely, however, that the former group will have additional professional qualifications.

Entry into the professional occupations generally involve intensive periods of educational investment which span a wide range of disciplines and draw in individuals with backgrounds in science, technology, health, teaching and other areas. SOC specifies that Group 2, 'professional occupations' require a degree or equivalent. According to the IER estimates, shown in Table 4.1, in 1989 approximately two-thirds of these professionals held degrees and of the four types of occupations contained in this Major Group, those engaged in the health professions were most likely to have degrees than other professionals, whilst a third of teaching professionals had non-degree teaching qualifications (IER 1992). In a similar way, SOC recommend that Group 3, 'associate professional and technical occupations' require a higher level of vocational qualification or post-graduate qualifications. Regarding the lower status occupations, SOC holds that Major Groups 4, 5 and 6 often require further vocational training, but of a lower level than that required for Group 3. Groups 7,8 and 9 typically do not require any formal or vocational qualifications, but rely on work-based training.

In this report we have set up a classification of seven groups, primarily based on the SOC Major Groups, which define the level of qualification 'required' for classes of occupations. The classification also takes into account the estimates from the 1992 IER report to give a more finely detailed breakdown of occupations, for example, those which require degree level qualifications. Our seven groups denoting qualification requirement are as follows;

1. Managerial occupations requiring no formal qualification.

2. Managerial occupations requiring a formal qualification (degree or higher vocational).

3. Occupations requiring a degree.

4. Occupations requiring teaching or nursing qualifications.

5. Occupations requiring vocational qualifications.

6. Occupations requiring a good standard of general education.

7. Occupations requiring no specified education.

Table 4.2 classifies SOC Sub-major groups by their qualification requirement using the seven classes above. Thus, all the professional occupations are deemed to require a degree, with the exception of the teaching professions, which allow non-degree teaching qualifications. Similarly, most of the associate professions require a degree, with the exception of health-related jobs where nursing qualifications are the norm. The Sub-major Groups of the lower six SOC Major Groups (clerical and other occupations) are not considered separately in Table 4.2, since their qualifications requirements are similar within Major Groups.

27

Table 4.1   BHPS 1991: Qualifications held by full-time employees by Standard Occupational Classification (Sub-major Groups)[a].

Sub-Major SOC	Degree row %	Intermediate Qualifications row %	No Qualifications row %	Other V.Qualifications[b] row %
Managers and Administrators				
Corporate Managers and Administrators	26	24	18	
Managers/ Proprietors in Agriculture and Services	8	20	39	
Professionals				
Science and Engineering Professionals	61	23	6	
Health Professionals	80	8	6	
Teaching Professionals (teaching)	53	4	4	
				34
Other Professional Occupations	58	15	8	
Associate Professionals				
Science and Engineering Associate Professionals	42	32	8	
Health Associate Professionals (nursing)	6	10	15	
				51
Other Associate Professionals Occupations	30	25	14	

a   Row percentage presented, base figures not available.

b   Other V.qualifications refer to specific vocational ones, i.e., teaching, nursing.

Source: Labour Force Survey 1989 (IER 1992)

Utilisation of qualifications in the labour market

Table 4.3 shows the extent to which highly qualified men and women were using their qualifications in the labour market. Occupations are classified according to the level of qualifications required as in Table 4.2 above and occupations for those in full-time employment, part-time employment or self-employment are considered together. For our highly qualified sample with degrees we note that women, in general, appeared to be less likely to be in jobs which utilised their qualification than men; over half (n=195) of higher academic men were in jobs which required a degree (level 3), compared to only 35% (n=96) of women. Furthermore, a third (n=94) of higher academic women were in the teaching or nursing professions (which may, in some instances require a degree), compared to only 16% (n=63) of men.

We noted earlier that higher academic women were more likely to choose vocational teaching careers than men. In our sample, these women were less likely than men to be in higher status managerial jobs, whilst a marginally higher proportion of higher academic women 17% (n=46) were in jobs which do not require a degree, that is, in levels 5, 6 and 7, compared to higher academic men 15% (n=58). Within these lower status occupations requiring lower levels of education, higher academic women tended to be concentrated in the occupations requiring vocational qualifications, whilst a greater proportion of male higher academics were in occupations which do not require any formal higher qualifications 7% (n=27). A small proportion of the higher academic group were in managerial jobs requiring no formal qualifications (level 1). The figures suggest that men and women were equally likely to be in jobs for which they were over-qualified.

Table 4.2   BHPS 1991: SOC Sub-Major Groups classified according to level of qualifications required, using the 7-level classification[a]

SOC Major Group SOC Sub-major Group	Level of qualification required:
Managers and Administrators	
Corporate Managers and Administrators	Level 2
Managers/ Proprietors in Agriculture and Services	Level 1
Professionals	
Science and Engineering Professionals	Level 3
Health Professionals·	Level 3
Teaching Professionals	Level 4
Other Professional Occupations	Level 3
Associate Professionals and Technical Occupations	
Science and Engineering Associate Professionals	Level 3
Health Associate Professionals	Level 4
Other Associate Professionals	Level 3
Clerical and Secretarial Occupations	Level 5
Craft and Related Occupations	Level 6
Personal and Protective Service Occupations	Level 5
Sales Occupations	Level 6
Plant and Machine Operatives	Level 7
Other Occupations	Level 7

a   *Key to classes:*

Level 1	*Managerial occupations requiring no formal qualification.*	
Level 2	*Managerial occupations requiring formal qualifications (degree or higher vocational).*	
Level 3	*Occupations requiring a degree.*	
Level 4	*Occupations requiring teaching or nursing qualifications.*	
Level 5	*Occupations requiring vocational qualifications.*	
Level 6	*Occupations requiring a good standard of general education.*	
Level 7	*Occupations requiring no specified education.*	

Regarding the utilising of vocational qualifications, we observe a rather different gender pattern. Once more, we find equal proportions of men and women in managerial positions which do not specifically require any formal qualifications, but find significantly more men in occupations that typically require a degree. Almost a third (n=146) of the vocationally qualified men were in degree level jobs compared to only 10% (n=34) of the vocationaally qualified women. In this respect, women suffer discrimination, and Table 4.3 suggests that the majority of vocationally qualified women were in occupations which matched their qualification. Vocationally qualified men were, however, much more likely to be in low status jobs, which require basic or no formal qualifications; 28% (n=129) were in these types of occupations compared to only a small minority (6%, n=20) of their female counterparts.

Table 4.4 examines the occupational position of the vocationally qualified, to assess whether there is a differential effect of having 'A' level qualifications for men and women on their chances of being in higher status jobs[1]. For this group of men, having

Table 4.3   BHPS 1991: Occupations based on level of qualifications required for the highly qualified in paid employment by gender[a]

Women aged 20-59 and men aged 20-64 in paid employment

Occupations requiring level of qualifications[b]	Higher academic*		Higher VQ*		Less qualified*		All BHPS	
	Women	Men	Women	Men	Women	Men		
	%	%	%	%	%	%	Freq	%
Level 1	(1.9)	(2.0)	3.9	3.8	5.0	5.5	247	4.6
Level 2	11.3	16.3	4.9	19.0	3.1	9.3	448	8.4
Level 3	35.2	50.3	9.9	31.5	5.5	7.6	729	13.7
Level 4	34.7	16.4	47.7	7.7	1.8	(.2)	391	7.3
Level 5	13.3	6.0	27.8	10.0	50.5	15.3	1415	26.5
Level 6	(2.9)	6.9	2.7	22.5	15.2	33.3	1116	20.9
Level 7	(0.7)	(2.1)	3.1	5.5	18.8	28.8	985	18.5
Base = 100%	271	387	339	462	1768	2103	5331	

a   Column percentage calculated on the base figures shown.

b   Key to classes:

   Level 1   Managerial occupations requiring no formal qualification.

   Level 2   Managerial occupations requiring formal qualifications (degree or higher vocational).

   Level 3   Occupations requiring a degree.

   Level 4   Occupations requiring teaching or nursing qualifications.

   Level 5   Occupations requiring vocational qualifications.

   Level 6   Occupations requiring a good standard of general education.

   Level 7   Occupations requiring no specified education.

66 cases with missing information are excluded; 12 for highly qualified; 55 for low qualified.

Brackets denote cell sizes less than 10 cases.

*   Sig. <.000.

'A' levels makes some difference to their occupational standing; almost a quarter of men with 'A' levels 24% (n=28) were in managerial jobs requiring higher qualifications compared to only 17% (n=58) of men without 'A' levels. Furthermore, men with 'A' levels were much less likely to be in the lower two occupational levels (levels 6 and 7) than those without 'A' levels (32% compared to 15.6%). Having 'A' levels does not, however, appear to make any difference to gaining entry into managerial jobs.

Table 4.4 suggests that women with vocational qualifications do not appear to benefit from having 'A' levels to the same degree as their male equivalents. Regardless of 'A' level status, half of these women were in nursing or teaching jobs, whilst only 5% more of those holding 'A' levels were in degree level jobs and marginally more were in occupations requiring lower level vocational qualifications (level 5). These level 5 occupations show a large gender difference for the group without

'A' levels, where we see a 22% difference between men and women. This compares with only a 9% difference for the group holding 'A' levels. A last observation concerns the number of men and women in the lowest status occupations (levels 6 and 7), requiring basic or no qualifications: of those without 'A' levels, men were far more likely to be in these lower two levels of occupations than women (32% compared to 7%).

Table 4.5 gives a further breakdown of type of qualification held by our highly qualified sample according to their present occupation, based on the level of qualification required. To those with teaching qualifications, we see that over two-thirds (n=54) of women were currently using their qualifications in teaching positions, whilst only one-third of the small number of men with teaching qualifications were (n=13). Whereas women with teaching qualifications who were not currently engaged in teaching positions were mostly (n=54)

Table 4.4 **BHPS 1991: Occupations based on level of qualifications required for men and women with higher vocational qualifications (non-degree) in paid employment by 'A' level status[a]**

Women aged 20-59 and men aged 20-64 with higher vocational qualifications

Occupations requiring level of qualifications[b]	Without 'A' levels*		With 'A' levels*		All with higher VQ	
	Women	Men	Women	Men		
	%	%	%	%	Freq	%
Level 1	(3.4)	3.8	(4.7)	(3.8)	31	3.9
Level 2	(4.2)	17.3	(6.1)	24.1	105	13.1
Level 3	8.4	30.9	12.7	33.3	179	22.3
Level 4	46.0	7.1	50.7	9.5	197	24.6
Level 5	30.8	8.7	22.6	13.7	141	17.6
Level 6	(2.3)	26.2	(3.2)	11.6	113	14.1
Level 7	4.9	6.0	-	(4.0)	36	4.5
Base = 100%	216	344	123	118	801	

a Column percentage calculated on the base figures shown.

b Key to classes - see Table 4.3.

6 cases with missing information are excluded.

Brackets denote cell sizes less than 10 cases.

* Sig. <.000.

found in lower level 5 jobs requiring only lower vocational qualifications, men tended to be in higher status jobs requiring a degree (n=8). Nursing qualifications largely appeared to be utilised for both men and women's current jobs with 62% (n=99) of women with nursing qualifications being in health related jobs. However, a quarter of qualified nurses were in lower status jobs (level 5) which required a lower level of vocational qualification than they held. Whilst, the number of men with nursing qualifications is small, over 80% (n=17) were in jobs matching their qualifications, suggesting they do better in their careers pursuits.

The group with higher BTEC/City and Guilds equivalent qualifications showed a greater gender differentiation. Although comparatively few women had this type of qualification, over half of these qualified women (n=27) were in occupations for which a higher BTEC/City and Guilds equivalent is probably a requirement, that is, primarily clerical or secretarial jobs. A fifth of women qualified to this level (n=11) were in jobs which normally require a degree. For the significant number of men holding an advanced BTEC/City and Guilds qualification, 38% (n=89) were currently in lower status jobs for which they were over qualified, and of these a fifth were in low status unskilled jobs requiring no formal

qualifications. Table 4.5 further suggests that of the vocationally qualified, a significantly greater proportion of men were in graduate level jobs, including managerial or administrative jobs, than women (47% compared to 28%).

The group with 'other' higher level vocational qualifications, that is, those who did not have a degree, teaching, nursing or higher BTEC/City and Guilds equivalent, tended to be concentrated in the higher status occupations. As we noted earlier, this group constitute a heterogeneous group of qualified men and women, but mostly men, and largely contain those have chartered status or who are members of recognised institutes. It is therefore not surprising that we find them in high status jobs. Table 4.5 suggests that 44% (n=52) of men with these 'other' qualifications were in occupations requiring a degree (level 3) compared to only 24% (n=11) of women, suggesting that men find it easier to enter the professional or associate professional occupations than women without the required formal academic qualifications. Over three times as many women than men with these qualifications were in level 5 occupations requiring lower level qualifications (33% and 10% respectively), whilst more men than women were in corporate managerial or administrative jobs (29% compared to 21%).

31

Table 4.5 **BHPS 1991: Occupations based on level of qualifications required for highly qualified men and women in paid employment by type of qualification held[a]**

Men aged 20-64 and women aged 20-59 in paid employment

| Occupations requiring level of qualifications[b] | Higher qualifications held | | | | | | |
| | Degree | Teaching | Nursing | BTEC /C&G | Other higher VQ | All | |
	%	%	%	%	%	Freq	%
*Women**							
Class 1	(1.9)	(5.5)	(1.9)	(7.4)	(3.8)	18	3.0
Class 2	11.3	(2.1)	(1.1)	(6.8)	(21.0)	47	7.7
Class 3	35.2	(5.8)	(4.5)	20.6	24.4	129	21.2
Class 4	34.7	65.4	61.7	(4.3)	16.3	256	41.9
Class 5	13.3	15.7	25.0	51.5	32.6	131	21.4
Class 6	(2.9)	(2.8)	(1.2)	(7.4)	(1.9)	17	2.8
Class 7	(.7)	(2.6)	(4.6)	(2.0)	-	12	2.0
Base = 100%	271	82	160	52	45	610	
*Men**							
Class 1	(2.0)	(5.6)	-	4.0	(3.5)	26	3.0
Class 2	16.3	(6.4)	-	17.9	28.7	151	17.8
Class 3	50.3	(21.3)	(4.0)	28.7	44.3	341	40.1
Class 4	16.4	36.2	82.5	(1.2)	(2.1)	99	11.7
Class 5	6.0	(12.9)	-	10.1	10.5	70	8.2
Class 6	6.9	(10.7)	(3.5)	30.7	9.0	131	15.4
Class 7	(2.1)	(6.9)	-	7.2	(1.8)	33	3.9
Base = 100%	387	36	20	289	118	850	

a   *Column percentage calculated on the base figures shown.*

b   *Key to classes - see Table 4.3.*

12 cases with missing information are excluded.

Brackets denote cell sizes less than 10 cases.

*   *Sig. <.000.*

Footnote to Section 4

1. The academically qualified are excluded from this table, since 82% of them have 'A' levels.

Section 5

Earnings and occupational status of highly qualified men and women

In this section we compare characteristics of job status and pay of highly qualified men and women.

Gross pay from employment

The BHPS questionnaire asks respondents, who are employees, for their most recent gross and net pay and then confirms whether this amount was the respondent's usual pay. Table 5.1 sets out the distribution of monthly gross pay for the sample of full-time and part-time employees and the self-employed. The amount of missing information for gross usual (or last), pay for full-time and part-time employees is in the order of 8%, but rises to over a third for the self-employed. For this report, no attempt has been made to impute earnings for individuals with missing information. Instead they are considered in a separate category rather than being omitted, which is therefore greatly heterogeneous in terms of earnings.

Table 5.1 reports earnings quartiles based on the whole sample of BHPS employees calculated separately for each employment status (full-time, part-time, self-employed). Considering the academically qualified in full-time employment first, we note that 23% more men than women were earning in the top quartile (63% compared to 40%). Almost a quarter of higher academic women in full-time jobs (24%, n=46) were found in the lowest two quartiles compared to only 15% (n=43) of their male counterparts. Furthermore, we observe a distinct inequality between the earnings of graduate men and women who are part-time or self-employed, with over 80% (n=21) of higher academic males in part-time jobs earning in the highest quartile compared to only half (n=27) of women. Similarly, of the self-employed, 13% more higher academic men earned in the top quartile than did equivalent women. However, it should noted that the numbers in these groups are small, and the differences are therefore not statistically significant.

For the vocationally qualified a similar yet more pronounced picture of gender inequality emerges. First it is evident that the earnings of this group were proportionally lower than those for the academically qualified sample. Of full-time employees, we note that vocationally trained men were over twice as likely to earn in the top quartile than women (45% compared to 18%). Furthermore, men in this top quartile outnumbered the proportion of women with degrees, but not men with degrees. Therefore, although women holding degrees were twice as likely to earn in the top quartile than their vocationally trained counterparts, they earned less than men with vocational qualifications. A significant proportion of the vocationally qualified women (19%, n=42) had a monthly gross pay in the bottom quartile, of less than £749, whilst the corresponding figure for men was only 5% (n=18).

Difference in pay for men and women in part-time employment cannot be suitably addressed with this sample given that the number of vocationally qualified men in part-time jobs is too small. However, of the 94 vocationally trained women in part-time occupations, approximately half (n=49) earned in the top pay quartile, rivalling the number of women with degrees. Similarly, in this report we cannot realistically assess gender differences in self-employed pay for the vocationally qualified due to the small number of self-employed women together with the overall high incidence of missing data. A third of the vocationally qualified sample of self-employed men reported receiving a monthly gross income in the top quartile (£1,549 or more), this proportion actually being greater than for self-employed graduate men.

Age clearly has a strong positive association with employment income. We might envisage a more evenly balanced situation for younger graduates in full-time jobs given moves towards equal opportunities over the last two decades. Tables 5.2 and 5.3 examine earnings differences for highly qualified men and women in full-time employment within age groups. In Table 5.2 it is noted that 18% more women over 35 years earned in the top quartile compared to their younger counterparts. For highly qualified men, the pattern suggests that earnings peak in the middle age range 35-44, with almost 70% earning in the top quartile after which the proportion drops to 60%. Nevertheless, we continue to observe a significant gender inequality in gross earnings from employment regardless of age. Gender differences in pay are most marked for the middle age group, of whom almost twice as many men earn over £1,452 a month than women (69% and 38% respectively). The difference for the younger and older age groups is less, 20%, but still significantly different.

Table 5.1 BHPS 1991: Usual gross earnings per month of highly qualified men and women in paid employment[a]

Women aged 20-59 and men aged 20-64 in paid employment

Monthly usual gross pay	Higher academic		Higher VQ		All BHPS employed			
	Women	Men	Women	Men	Women	Men	All	
	%	%	%	%	%	%	Freq	%
Full-time employees[b]	*		*		*			
< £749	11.1	6.0	19.3	4.9	39.4	13.1	821	22.7
£750 - £1031	13.0	8.9	24.4	11.6	23.2	22.5	824	22.8
£1032 - £1451	28.8	15.4	31.2	28.3	17.7	25.6	823	22.7
£1452+	40.3	62.9	18.3	45.2	11.8	28.9	822	22.7
Unstated	6.9	6.7	6.7	10.1	7.8	10.0	334	9.2
Base = 100%	190	291	223	367	1318	2306	3624	
Part-time employees[c]	ns		ns		*			
< £180	(16.8)	(3.8)	11.8	(29.8)	24.5	8.7	224	22.9
£181 - £297	(12.8)	-	11.8	(8.6)	23.9	10.2	220	22.5
£298 - £453	(13.1)	(8.0)	13.7	(8.6)	24.1	11.5	223	22.8
£454+	53.5	80.8	52.1	(25.0)	19.5	54.1	225	23.0
Unstated	(3.9)	(7.6)	10.6	(25.0)	8.0	15.4	86	
Base = 100%	51	26	94	12	881	98	979	
Self-employed[d]	ns		ns		*			
< £380	(19.1)	(12.8)	(41.5)	(1.3)	34.6	9.0	97	14.9
£381 - £833	(8.1)	15.7	(10.3)	15.9	14.0	16.2	102	15.7
£834 - £1548	(16.3)	(12.0)	-	15.2	(5.1)	18.1	99	15.2
£1549+	16.3	28.8	-	32.9	(4.9)	18.7	101	15.5
Unstated	39.2	30.7	(48.2)	34.7	41.4	38.0	252	38.8
Base = 100%	25	61	19	73	148	502	650	

a   Column percentage calculated on the base figures shown.

b   Earned quartiles based on the sample of all full-time employees.

c   Earned quartiles based on the sample of all part-time employees.

d   Earned quartiles based on the sample of all self-employees.

Brackets denote cell sizes less than 10 cases.

*   Sig. < .000.

ns sig = not significant

Younger women do especially badly compared to their male counterparts, with over a fifth of women (n=48) earning in the bottom quartile compared to only 8% (n=24) of younger men. Although mature highly qualified women were less likely to receive a monthly gross income below that of younger women, they were still over twice as likely to be in this bracket compared to their older male counterparts.

Table 5.3 examines mean gross pay for full-time employees by age. For the academic group the gender difference in mean income rises with age from £297 for the younger age group, to £327 for middle age group to £500 for those over 45. For the vocationally qualified group the corresponding gender differences peak for the 35-44 age group - £221, £713 and £527 respectively.

Table 5.2   BHPS 1991: Usual gross earnings per month of highly qualified men and women in full-time employment by age[a]

Women aged 20-59 and men aged 20-64

Monthly usual gross pay[b]	20-34		35-44		45+		All BHPS employees	
	Women	Men	Women	Men	Women	Men		
	%	%	%	%	%	%	Freq	%
Full-time employees	*		*		*			
< £749	21.3	8.1	9.7	2.7	7.8	3.7	821	22.7
£750-1031	23.2	15.2	12.7	6.2	16.3	6.7	824	22.8
£1032-1451	30.2	29.3	30.2	16.2	29.9	18.1	823	22.7
£1452+	20.2·	40.2	38.1	68.5	38.1	57.9	822	22.7
Unstated	7.3	5.2	9.4	6.4	7.9	13.7	334	9.2
Base = 100%	224	297	100	196	89	164	3624	

a   Column percentage calculated on the base figures shown.

b   Earned quartiles based on the sample of all full-time employees.

*   Sig. <.000.

Table 5.3   BHPS 1991: Mean usual gross earnings per month of highly qualified full-time employees by gender and age[a]

Women aged 20-59 and men aged 20-64

Mean monthly usual gross pay[b]	20-34		35-44		45+		All ages		
	Women	Men	Women	Men	Women	Men	Women	Men	All
	£	£	£	£	£	£	£	£	£
*Academically qualified**									
Mean earnings	1291.2	1588.1	1638.8	1965.6	1541.7	2042.1	1421.3	1805.9	1654.2
Base N	102	126	45	87	30	58	177	27 1	448
*Vocationally qualified**									
Mean earnings	1081.2	1302.3	1206.0	1919.5	1301.1	1828.4	1163.9	1616.6	1441.4
Base N	110	149	46	96	52	84	208	33 0	538
*All BHPS full-time employees**									
Mean earnings	932.0	1388.3	996.2	1227.8	920.8	1432.3	945.0	1388.3	1224.7
Base N	148	110	96	46	84	52	1214	2 076	3290

a   Column percentage calculated on the base figures shown.

b   Mean income calculated for full-time employees only.

334 cases with missing are excluded.

*   Sig. <.000.

Table 5.4 BHPS 1991: Managerial or supervisory responsibilities of highly qualified men and women in full-time paid employment[a]

Women aged 20-59 and men aged 20-64

Managerial or supervisory duties	Higher academic		Higher VQ*		All BHPS** (f-time emp)			
	Women	Men	Women	Men	Women	Men	All	
	%	%	%	%	%	%	Freq	%
Manager	39.5	50.0	22.9	39.9	19.1	23.7	797	22.1
Forman/Supervisor	17.6	15.7	36.6	22.5	22.4	21.0	776	21.5
Neither manager or supervisor	42.9	34.3	40.5	37.6	58.5	55.3	2038	56.4
Base = 100%	190	289	222	367	1314	2299	3613	

a   Column percentage calculated on the base figures shown.

14 cases with missing information are excluded.

*   Sig. <.000.

**   Sig. <.01.

Table 5.5 BHPS 1991: Contractual status of present job of highly qualified men and women in full-time paid employment[a]

Women aged 20-59 and men aged 20-64

Contractual status of job	Higher academic*		Higher VQ*		All BHPS** (f-time emp)			
	Women	Men	Women	Men	Women	Men	All	
	%	%	%	%	%	%	Freq	%
Permanent	87.1	93.2	94.3	97.1	94.0	96.1	3449	95.3
Seasonal, temporary or casual	5.9	(1.4)	-	(1.6)	3.2	1.9	86	2.4
Contract or fixed period of time	7.0	5.4	5.7	(1.3)	2.8	2.0	83	2.3
Base = 100%	190	290	222	366	1316	2302	3618	

a   Column percentage calculated on the base figures shown.

9 cases with missing information are excluded.

Brackets denote cell sizes less than 10 cases.

*   Sig. <.005.

**   Sig. <.05.

Contractual status and managerial responsibilities

Table 5.4 and 5.5 display the contractual status and managerial responsibilities for highly qualified employees. A greater proportion of higher academic men (50%, n=145) reported having managerial duties in their jobs compared to highly qualified women (40%, n=75), although the difference is not statistically significant. For the vocationally qualified, only just over a fifth (n=51) of women reported having managerial duties compared to 40% (n=146) of men. Roughly equal proportions of men and women with academic qualifications had supervisory duties in their current jobs, whereas women with vocational qualifications were more likely to be supervisors than their male counterparts. This situation mostly reflects the types of occupations in which the majority of vocationally trained women were in, such as nursing and teaching jobs, where supervisory responsibilities may be considered to be inherent features of the jobs.

When we examine the contractual status of current full-time jobs for the highly qualified, in Table 5.4, we find a greater proportion of our vocationally qualified sample than the group with degrees describing themselves as being in permanent jobs. Of all the groups, although the numbers are small, academically qualified women were most likely to hold seasonal or temporary jobs, and were also more likely to be in fixed term contract jobs. The numbers of highly qualified men in seasonal or temporary jobs was insignificant, but more men with degrees were in fixed term contract jobs than other men.

Section 6

Comparing individual, household and employment characteristics of highly qualified and less qualified women

The first sections of this report have been predominantly concerned with the employment situation of highly qualified women in comparison with men holding similar levels and types of qualifications. The following section is concerned primarily with women only. Women holding above 'A' level qualifications, either academic called *'higher academic'* or vocational called *'higher vocational'*, are compared with women without such qualifications called *'less qualified'* according to their current employment status, their household circumstances, their attitudes to work and job satisfaction, caring responsibilities for children, the domestic division of labour and the employment characteristics of spouses for married and cohabiting women.

Individual and household characteristics

Table 6.1 gives the characteristics of all women of working age in the BHPS sample by the level and type of qualification held. Women with higher academic qualifications tended to be in the 20 to 34 year old age group, to be single and to have no dependent children. Of those with higher academic qualifications 52% (n=165) were aged between 20 and 34 years compared to 20% (n=64) of those aged 45 years and over. In addition 24% (n=75) of those holding higher academic qualifications were single and 68% (n=216) were married or cohabiting compared to 14% (n=371) and 74% (n=2049) respectively of women with 'A' level or below qualifications. Of women with higher academic qualifications 64% (n=204) had no dependent children compared to 52% (n=1444) of women with less qualifications. Women with higher vocational qualifications were also concentrated in the younger age range although the distribution was more even than for women with higher academic qualifications. There was also a less marked relationship with marital status and the number of dependent children for women with higher vocational qualifications than for those with higher academic qualifications.

Less qualified women were most likely to be in the 45 and over age group, to be married and to have dependent children.

There were also marked differences in current employment status depending on the type of qualification held. In the BHPS sample 68% (n=2392) of women aged between 20 and 59 years were in paid employment of some kind and 32% were not in employment.[1] Of the women with high academic qualifications 86% (n=319) were in employment compared to 80% (n=342) of those with high vocational qualifications and 65% (n=1777) of those with less qualifications.

While those in paid employment holding higher qualifications, (either academic or vocational) were most likely to be found in the younger age range of between 20 and 34 years, similar percentages of those not in paid employment were also in the younger age range (Table 6.2). Of higher academically qualified women in employment, 50% (n=137) were aged between 20 and 34 years compared with 43% (n=58) of the higher qualified, (either academic or vocational), who were not in paid employment. Non-employed women with high qualifications were also more likely to be married than women holding similar qualifications who were in employment. However it is the presence of dependent children which has the most marked effect on whether highly qualified women are in paid employment or not. Of the women in employment 68% (n=186) of those with higher academic qualifications and 62% (n=212) of those with higher vocational qualifications had no dependent children. This compared to 43% (n=58) of highly qualified women not in employment who had no dependent children. It should also be noted that a similar relationship is apparent for less qualified women even though this is not as marked. Of the less qualified women in employment 58% (n=1038) had no dependent children compared to 42% (n=406) of less qualified women who were not in employment.

Table 6.1   BHPS 1991: Characteristics of all women by level and type of qualification[b]

	Higher academic %	Higher VQ %	All highly qualified %	Less qualified %	All women Freq	All women %
*Age in years**						
20-34	51.7	42.6	46.4	41.2	1483	42.3
35-44	28.2	26.7	27.3	26.3	929	26.5
45-59	20.1	30.9	26.3	32.5	1091	31.2
*Marital status ♦***						
Married	67.7	76.0	72.6	74.4	2592	74.0
Single	23.5	14.7	18.4	13.5	509	14.5
Other	8.5	9.3	8.9	12.1	401	11.5
Missing	0.0	0.2	0.1	0.0	1	0.0
*Current employment***						
In employment	85.6	79.5	82.2	64.5	2392	68.3
Not in employment	14.4	20.2	17.8	35.5	1111	31.7
*Number of children <16 in household***						
None	63.9	58.6	60.9	52.4	1900	54.2
One	15.4	16.7	16.1	20.0	670	19.1
Two	16.0	17.7	17.0	19.1	652	18.6
Three	3.8	4.7	4.3	6.8	221	6.3
Four or more	0.6	2.6	1.7	1.7	60	1.7
Age of youngest child						
Two or under	13.8	15.6	14.8	14.8	517	14.8
3-4 years	2.8	4.4	3.8	6.6	211	6.0
5-12 years	14.7	14.9	14.8	19.2	641	18.3
13-15 years	4.4	5.8	5.1	6.3	211	6.0
No children	64.6	59.1	61.4	53.0	1920	54.8
Missing	0.0	0.2	0.1	0.1	3	0.1
Base = 100%	319	430	749	2354	3503	

VQ refers to vocational qualifications.

a   *Column percentages calculated on the base figures shown.*

b   *Women aged 20 - 59 years.*

*   *Sig. <.01.*

**   *Sig. <.001.*

♦   *'Married' includes cohabiting.*

'Other' includes widowed, divorced and separated.

Table 6.2   BHPS 1991: Characteristics of women by current employment and level of qualification held[a]

	In employment			Not in employment		All women	
	Higher academic	Higher VQ	Less qualified	All highly qualified	Less qualified		
	%	%	%	%	%	Freq	%
Age in years							
20-34	50.2	44.4	39.0	43.3	45.2	1483	42.3
35-44	27.8	26.3	29.4	29.1	20.7	929	26.2
45-59	22.0	29.2	31.6	27.6	34.1	1091	31.2
Marital status◆[b]							
Married	66.3	73.7	76.6	82.1	70.4	2592	74.0
Single	24.5	17.0	13.5	9.7	13.4	509	14.5
Other	9.2	9.4	9.9	7.5	16.2	401	11.5
Missing	0.0	0.3	0.0	0.0	0.0	1	0.0
No. of children <16 household							
None	68.1	62.0	58.4	43.3	41.6	1900	54.2
One	14.7	16.1	19.2	19.4	21.3	670	19.1
Two	13.9	16.7	16.5	23.9	23.7	652	18.6
Three	2.6	4.4	5.0	7.5	10.2	221	6.3
Four or more	0.4	1.2	0.9	6.0	3.3	60	1.7
Age of youngest in household							
Two or under	8.4	12.6	8.4	33.6	26.4	517	14.8
3-4 years	2.6	4.1	4.6	6.0	10.4	211	6.0
5-12 years	15.4	15.5	20.5	11.9	17.0	641	18.3
13-15 years	4.8	5.6	7.6	5.2	3.9	211	6.0
No children	68.9	62.6	58.9	43.3	42.4	1920	54.8
Missing	0.0	0.0	0.1	0.7	0.0	3	0.1
Base + 100%	273	342	1777	134	977	3503	

VQ refers to vocational qualifications.

a   *Column percentages calculated on the base figures shown.*

b   *Women aged 20 - 59 years.*

*   *Sig. <.01.*

**   *Sig. <.001.*

◆   *'Married' includes cohabiting.*

'Other' includes widowed, divorced and separated.

Employment characteristics

Table 6.3 describes the job characteristics of women who were in current paid employment by the level and type of qualification held. There was no significant relationship between qualifications held by women by whether they were an employee or self-employed, although those with higher vocational qualifications were more likely than those with higher academic qualifications to be employees. There was a marked relationship between level of qualifications held and occupation with 74% (n=451) of the higher qualified being in managerial, professional or associate professional occupations compared to 16% (n=274) of the less qualified. Whether the higher qualification was academic or vocational also affected the type of occupation held by women with 83% (n=225) of those with higher academic qualifications being in managerial/professional occupations compared to 66% (n=225) of those with higher vocational qualifications. Similarly a higher percentage of women with higher vocational qualifications, 30% (n=103), were found in clerical, craft, personal service and sales occupations than women with higher academic qualifications, 16% (n=44) of whom were in these types of occupations. When we look at the usual number of hours worked per week, 72% (n=445) of highly qualified women worked 30 hours or more per week compared to 56% (n=987) of less qualified women. The type of higher qualification again has an effect, with women with academic qualifications being more likely than those with vocational qualifications to work 40 hours or more per week.

The levels of monthly earnings reflect both the types of occupations held by highly qualified women and the number of hours they worked. However, there was a marked difference in monthly earnings depending on whether they were an employee or self-employed, possibly due to the irregular hours or intermittent nature of some self-employed occupations. In the case of highly qualified women employees, 18% (n=91) were in the bottom earnings quartile[2] compared to 54% (n=14) of self-employed highly qualified women. In contrast 32% (n=163) of highly qualified women employees were in the top earnings quartile compared to 15% (n=4) of self-employed women with similar qualifications[3]. The majority of less qualified women employees were in the bottom earnings quartile with 54% (n=809) being in this category. For highly qualified women employees there were also marked differences in earnings level depending on whether the qualification held was academic or vocational in type. Overall women employees with higher vocational qualifications were more likely to be in

the bottom three earnings quartiles than women with higher academic qualifications. In total 79% (n=224) of women employees with higher vocational qualifications were in the bottom three earnings quartiles compared to 54% (n=120) of women with higher academic qualifications. Women employees with higher academic qualifications clearly had the highest earnings with 47% (n=104) of these women being in the top earnings quartile compared to 21% (n=59) of women employees with vocational qualifications and only 4% (n=54) of less qualified women.

Opportunities for promotion and training

In the BHPS survey employees were asked whether they had opportunities for promotion in their current job. Of the 2,200 women employees aged between 20-59, 41% (n=978) said they did have opportunities for promotion in their current job (see Table 6.4a). As might be expected given the occupations they held, highly qualified women were more likely to say they had promotion opportunities than less qualified women, with 60% (n=335) of the highly qualified giving this response compared to 39% (n=643) of less qualified women employees. In addition, women employees with higher academic qualifications were more likely than those with vocational qualifications or with less qualifications to say they had opportunities for promotion in their current job. Of women employees with higher academic qualifications 64% (n=154) said they had opportunities for promotion in their current job compared to 57% (n=181) of those with vocational qualifications and 39% (n=643) of the less qualified. The career structures within occupations clearly differ in many respects according to the level of qualification. This is apparent when we cross-classify occupation by qualification held and control for whether women have promotion opportunities in their current job (see Table 6.4a). Of those saying they had promotion opportunities 40% (n=389) were in managerial, professional or associate professional occupations compared to 33% (n=320) in clerical or craft occupations and 17% (n=161) in personal service or sales occupations.

Whether respondents had opportunities for promotion also varied by gender. Regardless of the level of qualification held, men were more likely than women to have opportunities for promotion with 59% (n=1428) of male employees saying they had promotion opportunities compared to 44% (n=978) of female employees. Table 6.4b gives a breakdown of promotion opportunities for male employees. There were statistically significant

Table 6.3   BHPS 1991: Employment characteristics of women in employment by level and type of qualification held[a]

	Higher academic	Higher VQ	All highly qualified	Less qualified	All women	
	%	%	%	%	Freq	%
Employment status						
Employee	88.3	92.7	90.7	92.4	2200	92.0
Self-employed	11.4	6.7	8.9	7.3	125	7.7
Inapplicable	0.0	0.6	0.3	0.3	7	0.3
Base = 100%	273	342	615	1777	2392	
*Occupation***						
Man/Professional	83.0	66.4	73.9	15.5	724	30.4
Clerical/Craft	11.1	16.8	14.1	38.6	768	32.3
Personal/Sales	5.2	13.6	10.0	27.1	541	22.7
Plant/Other	0.7	3.2	2.0	18.8	346	14.5
Base = 100%	271	339	610	1768	2378	
*Usual weekly hours worked***						
<16	7.0	14.0	10.7	17.2	372	15.5
16-29	13.9	15.5	14.8	25.8	549	23.0
30-39	52.7	55.6	54.3	41.9	1078	45.1
40 and over	24.2	12.9	18.0	13.7	354	14.8
missing/DK	1.8	2.0	2.1	1.5	39	1.6
Base = 100%	273	342	615	1777	2392	
*Usual monthly earnings - employees only***[c]						
<£542	12.1	22.5	17.9	54.3	900	45.1
£542-875	15.2	23.6	19.9	29.6	541	27.1
£876-1321	26.5	32.7	30.0	12.4	337	16.9
£1321+	46.6	20.8	32.1	3.6	218	10.9
Base = 100%	223	284	507	1490	1997	
Monthly earnings self-employed[c]						
<380	37.5	80.0	53.8	62.5	53	59.4
381-833	12.5	20.0	15.4	28.1	22	24.1
834-1548	25.0	0.0	15.4	6.3	8	8.4
1549+	25.0	0.0	15.4	4.7	7	8.1
Base = 100%[b]	16	10	26	64	90	

*   Sig. <01.

**   Sig. <001.

a   Women aged 20-59 in employment.

b   Column percentages calculated on the base figures shown.

c   Women with missing information excluded.

differences between men and women on whether they had opportunities for promotion after qualifications were controlled. Of all highly qualified men 70% (n=490) said they had opportunities for promotion in their current job and 55% (n=938) of less qualified men said the same. In addition whereas women holding an academic qualification were more likely than women with a vocational qualification to have opportunities for promotion, this relationship does not hold for men. For men the type of qualification held, either academic or vocational, made no difference to whether they had opportunities for promotion. When we compare the promotion prospects of less qualified men to those of women with higher vocational qualifications the distributions are very similar. Less qualified men were almost as likely to report having promotion possibilities as highly qualified women, 55% and 57% respectively. This suggests that while having a higher qualification is advantageous for women's promotion prospects when compared to less qualified women, having a higher qualification does not necessarily improve women's chances of promotion relative to men. Whether women have opportunities for promotion is dependent not only upon their qualifications but is also associated with the segregated nature of the labour market and issues of equality of opportunity for women in the workplace.

Table 6.4a   BHPS 1991: Whether has opportunity for promotion in current job - women employees only[a]

Promotion opportunities	Higher academic	Higher VQ	All highly qualified	Less qualified	All women employees	
	%	%	%	%	Freq	%
Whether has promotion opportunities						
Yes	63.7	57.0	60.0	39.2	978	40.9
No	33.9	42.3	38.6	59.4	1191	49.8
Missing/DK	2.2	0.7	1.4	1.5	31	1.3
Base = 100%	241	317	558	1642	2200	
Has promotion opportunities						
Occupation						
Man/professional	87.6	73.7	80.2	19.0	389	39.9
Clerical/craft	9.2	16.2	12.9	43.3	320	32.9
Personal/sales	3.3	6.7	5.2	22.3	161	16.5
Plant/other	0.0	3.4	1.8	15.4	105	10.8
Base = 100%	153	179	332	642	974	
No promotion opportunities						
Occupation						
Man/professional	78.0	57.5	65.4	9.9	237	20.0
Clerical/craft	12.2	19.4	16.4	37.9	404	34.0
Personal/sales	8.5	20.9	16.1	30.1	328	27.6
Plant/other	1.2	2.2	2.1	22.0	219	18.4
Base = 100%	82	134	216	972	1188	

a   *Women employees aged 20 - 59 years.*

Sig. <.001.

7 cases where occupation unable to be coded excluded.

43

Table 6.4b   BHPS 1991: Whether has opportunity for promotion in current job - male employees only[a]

Promotion opportunities	Higher academic	Higher VQ	All highly qualified	Less qualified	All men employees	
	%	%	%	%	Freq	%
Whether has promotion opportunities						
Yes	70.0	70.3	70.2	54.7	1428	59.2
No	29.3	28.6	28.9	43.8	953	39.5
Missing/DK	.8	1.1	.9	1.5	34	1.4
Base = 100%	318	381	699	1716	2415	
Has promotion opportunities						
Occupation						
Man/professional	83.6	66.4	74.9	23.9	586	41.2
Clerical/craft	11.1	20.4	16.2	35.6	411	28.9
Personal/sales	5.3	8.5	7.1	15.4	178	12.5
Plant/other	0.0	4.7	2.5	25.2	248	17.4
Base = 100%	222	267	489	934	1423	
No promotion opportunities						
Occupation						
Man/professional	83.4	52.4	66.6	16.6	258	27.2
Clerical/craft	4.9	35.7	21.5	36.8	318	33.6
Personal/sales	5.3	4.7	4.9	7.6	67	7.0
Plant/other	6.5	7.3	6.9	39.0	305	32.2
Base = 100%	93	109	202	747	948	

a   *Male employees aged 20 - 64 years.*
Sig. <.001.

All respondents in the BHPS survey were asked whether they had received any training or education in the previous year of either a non-job specific or job specific type[4]. In total only 12% (n=393) of women aged 20-59 said they had received training or education which was non-job specific in the past year. Although the majority, 64% (n=250) of those saying they had received this type of training or education were less qualified, the percentages within differing levels and type of education qualification held, indicate that those with higher qualifications were more likely to have undertaken non-job specific training or education in the past year. Of those women with higher academic qualifications 23% (n=69) said they had received training of this type compared to 18% (n=74) of women with higher

vocational qualifications and 9% (n=250) of the less qualified. Respondents who had done some training were also asked for the purpose of the training. In the case of non-job specific training they were asked if the training was to improve their skills in their current job; or to increase their skills in their current job, for example by learning new technology; to prepare them for a job or jobs they might do in the future and to develop their skills generally[5]. In all cases there were no statistically significant relationships between the reason for doing such training and the level and type of qualification currently held.

Employees who were in current employment were asked an additional question about any job-specific training they had taken as part of their present employment including the purpose of the training. Highly qualified women were more likely to have undertaken job-specific training than less qualified women. Overall 61% (n=340) of highly qualified women employees had done some form of job-specific training in the past year compared to 32% (n=536) of less qualified women (see Table 6.5a). Further, women with higher academic qualifications were more likely than those with higher vocational qualifications to have had job-specific training with 64% (n=155) of higher academically qualified women and 58% (n=185) of the vocationally qualified giving this response. The reasons for undertaking job-specific training included induction training to help them do their current job; to improve their skills in their current job; to increase their skills in their current job for example by learning new technology; to prepare them for a job or jobs they might do in the future and to develop their skills generally[6]. The only reason for which there was a statistically significant relationship with the level and type of qualification held was where training was to improve skills in the current job. In this case women with higher vocational qualifications were more likely to give this as a reason for doing the training than either academically qualified or less qualified women. Of those with higher vocational qualifications 86% (n=156) gave this as a reason compared to 81.9% (n=127) of the higher academically qualified and 76% (n=403) of the less qualified.

As with opportunites for promotion, gender was also a factor in whether job specific training had been undertaken in the past year (see Table 6.5b). Overall men were more likely than women to have had such training, 45% (n=1078) of men compared to 40% (n=871) of women. When the level of qualification is controlled significant differences between men and women persist for the less qualified. However gender differences in job specific training disappear where higher qualifications are held. In this respect the level of qualification held by women does appear to improve their access to job related training. However, it should also be remembered that this may be the result of the types of occupations held by women with higher qualifications. Managerial, professional and associate professional occupations could be expected to offer more training opportunities for women than the clerical or personal service occupations held by the majority of less qualified women.

The mean number of days spent in both non-job specific and job specific training by women also varied according to the level and type of qualification held and current employment status. Overall, a higher mean number of days had been spent in non-job specific training/education by all women than in job specific training (see Table 6.6). Not surprisingly those in current employment had spent a higher number of days on average doing job specific training than those not in employment at the time of interview. Conversely, women not in employment at the time of interview had spent a higher number of days doing non-job specific training or education. Highly qualified women had spent a higher mean number of days than less qualified women in job specific training but had spent less time on average in non-job specific training/education. On average, women with higher academic qualifications had spent the least time doing non-job specific training while women with higher vocational qualifications did not differ from less qualified women on the average days spent on this form of training. However, women with vocational qualifications had the highest mean number of days of job specific training when compared to other women[7].

Table 6.5a **BHPS 1991: Whether has undertaken job specific training in past year - women employees only[a]**

Training undertaken	Higher academic	Higher VQ	All highly qualified	Less qualified	All women employees	
	%	%	%	%	Freq	%
Whether has done training						
Yes	64.0	58.0	60.7	32.3	876	39.4
No	36.0	42.0	39.3	67.7	1346	60.6
Base = 100%	242	319	561	1661	2222	
Reason for training:						
Induction current job						
Yes	42.1	40.8	41.4	42.8	361	42.2
No	57.1	59.2	58.6	47.4	493	57.8
Base = 100%	152	179	331	523	854	
*Improve skills in current job***						
Yes	81.9	85.7	83.9	76.2	686	79.2
No	18.1	14.3	16.1	23.8	180	20.8
Base = 100%	155	182	337	529	866	
Increase skills for current job						
Yes	53.9	60.4	57.3	59.5	504	58.6
No	46.1	39.6	42.7	40.5	355	41.4
Base = 100%	154	182	336	523	859	
Preparation future jobs						
Yes	42.8	47.5	45.5	43.8	379	44.4
No	57.2	51.9	54.5	56.2	475	55.6
Base = 100%	152	181	333	521	854	
To develop skills generally						
Yes	71.9	76.7	74.4	76.2	645	75.5
No	28.1	23.9	25.6	23.8	210	24.5
Base[b] = 100%	153	180	333	522	855	

a   *Women 20 - 59 years.*

b   *Column percentages calculated on the base figures shown.*

**   *Sig. <.001.*

Table 6.5b   BHPS 1991: Whether has undertaken job specific training in past year - male employees only[a]

Training undertaken	Higher academic	Higher VQ	All highly qualified	Less qualified	All male employees	
	%	%	%	%	Freq	%
Whether has done training						
Yes	64.4	56.3	60.0	38.5	1078	44.7
No	35.6	43.7	40.0	61.5	1337	55.3
Base = 100%	318	381	699	1716	2415	
Reason for training:						
Induction current job						
Yes	34.7	31.6	33.1	41.5	399	38.2
No	65.3	68.4	66.9	58.5	645	61.8
Base = 100%	202	207	409	634	1043	
*Improve skills in current job**￼						
Yes	84.3	78.0	81.8	71.8	797	75.4
No	15.7	22.0	18.9	28.2	259	24.6
Base = 100%	203	212	415	641	1057	
Increase skills for current job						
Yes	58.4	61.9	60.2	65.8	671	63.6
No	41.6	38.1	39.8	34.2	384	36.4
Base = 100%	204	208	412	643	1055	
Preparation future jobs						
Yes	47.8	51.0	49.4	51.9	532	50.9
No	52.2	49.0	50.6	48.1	513	49.1
Base = 100%	204	210	414	631	1045	
To develop skills generally						
Yes	74.1	78.1	76.1	71.0	765	73.0
No	25.9	21.9	23.9	29.0	283	27.0
Base[b] = 100%	204	207	411	637	1048	

a   Men 20 - 64 years.

b   Column percentages calculated on the base figures shown.

**   Sig. <.001.

Table 6.6   BHPS 1991: Mean number of days spent on training/education in past year[a]

Training/education	Mean days spent[b]	Std.dev.	Valid cases
All women			1989
Non-job specific	22.46	51.57	
In current employment			1659
Non-job specific	19.78	46.67	
Job specific	8.19	17.78	
Not in current employment			330
Non-job specific	35.95	69.80	
Job specific	3.71	9.96	
All highly qualified			552
Non-job specific	20.47	40.94	
Job specific	9.22	20.12	
Academic qualifications			250
Non-job specific	17.38	35.41	
Job specific	8.74	16.88	
Vocational qualifications			302
Non-job specific	23.03	44.89	
Job specific	9.60	22.47	
Less qualified			1437
Non-job specific	23.23	55.10	
Job specific	6.77	15.32	

a   *Women 20 - 59 years.*

b   *Means based on number of respondents who had undertaken training in the previous year. Where a number of days could not be computed or were missing these values were set to zero.*

Continuity of employment

The first wave of the BHPS survey collected a retrospective history of the previous year's employment for all respondents. It is not possible to address the longitudinal questions surrounding the continuity of employment of highly qualified women with these data. However they do provide a starting point for the analysis which is to follow in Phase 2 of this project when two waves of panel data and a lifetime employment status history will be available.

The data from Wave 1 of the survey suggest that highly qualified women, and in particular academically qualified women, may be more mobile in terms of their employment than other groups of women. Table 6.7 suggests that of those who were in paid employment and who held higher academic qualifications 63% (n=152) had been in their current job for over one year compared to 69% (n=222) of those with higher vocational qualifications and 72% (n=1192) of the less qualified. However when we look further at the number of employers of the past year in conjunction with the number of employment spells over the past year the pattern for the highly qualified is one of a mixture of continuity and mobility in employment. Overall highly qualified women were less likely to have had no employment spells in the past year than less qualified women, with 14% (n=103) of highly qualified women having no spells of employment, compared to 29% (n=811) of less qualified women. Further, 68% (n=511) of highly qualified women had only one employment spell over the past year, compared to 59% (n=1629) of less qualified women. However a higher percentage of the highly qualified had two employment spells when compared to less qualified women suggesting that some highly qualified women may find it easier to move in and out of employment than the less qualified. Of the highly qualified, 16% (n=117) had two employment spells compared to 10% (n=265) of less qualified women. A similar pattern is found when the number of employers over the past year is examined with 75% (n=564) of highly qualified women having had one employer over the past year compared to 62% (n=1706) of less qualified women. On the number of unemployment spells over the past year there were no statistically significant differences between the highly qualified and the less qualified but there were marked differences on the number of inactive spells in the past year. Of the highly qualified, 75% (n=563) had no inactive spells in the past year compared to 63% (n=1742) of the less qualified, further 23% (n=99) of highly qualified women had one inactive spell compared to 35% (n=961) of less qualified women.

A further dimension of women's continuity of employment is the length of employment and non-employment spells they experience. Table 6.8 cross-classifies women's employment at the time of interview by whether or not they were in paid employment one year previous to interview[8]. The majority of women had not moved between being in paid employment and not being in paid employment since the previous year. However, 8% (n=198) had moved from employment to non-employment while 15% (n=173) of those not in employment one year previous to interview had moved into paid employment. When the level and type of qualification are controlled a higher percentage of highly qualified women moved from non-employment to employment when compared to less qualified women. In total 29% (n=44) of highly qualified women had moved into employment from non-employment in the past year compared to 13% (n=129) of less qualified women. However it was those with higher academic qualifications who were most likely to have moved from non-employment to employment when compared with women holding higher vocational qualifications. Of the higher academically qualified who were not in employment one year previous to interview 46% (n=29) had moved into paid employment compared to 17% (n=15) of those with vocational qualifications[9]. This suggests that it is not only the level of qualification held but the type of qualification which affects women's mobility within the labour market as well as movements in and out of paid employment.

Employment characteristics of spouse

Where women were married or cohabiting we can also examine the employment situation of their spouse/partner according to the level and type of qualification held by the woman. It might be expected for example that highly qualified women with professional jobs for example would tend to marry or have a partner with a similar level of qualifications and/or employment characteristics. In the first instance highly qualified women were less likely than less qualified women to have a spouse/partner who was not in paid employment. Table 6.9 shows that of the highly qualified women 10% (n=53) had a non-employed spouse/partner compared to 16% (n=316) of less qualified women. Second, the majority of highly qualified women, 61% (n=279) had a spouse/partner in a managerial, professional or associate professional occupation. The majority of highly qualified women also had a spouse/partner with earnings in the top income quartile with 61% (n=229) of highly qualified women being in this situation compared to 39% (n=479) of less qualified women. As has been found throughout the analysis there were also marked differences within the highly qualified group depending on whether the woman's higher qualification was academic or vocational. As Table 6.9 shows, women with higher academic qualifications were more likely than those with vocational qualifications to have a spouse/partner in a managerial, professional or associate professional occupation. Of the higher academically qualified women 75% (n=139) had a spouse/partner in these types of occupations compared to 52% (n=140) of women with higher vocational qualifications.

A similar pattern is found when we look at the spouse/partner's earnings with 68% (n=104) of highly qualified women having a spouse/partner with monthly earnings in the top earnings quartile compared to 56% (n=125) of women with vocational qualifications. There was no statistically significant relationship between the level of qualification held by the woman and her spouse/partner's hours of work. The overwhelming majority of men who were in employment worked full-time i.e. 30 hours or more per week with only 3% (n=58) working less than 30 hours per week.

It is also interesting to note that when we control for the employment status of the woman the same relationships hold to a large extent (see Table 6.10). Highly qualified women continued to be more likely than less qualified women to have a spouse/partner in paid employment and for the partner to be in a relatively high status occupation with relatively high earnings regardless of their own employment status.

Table 6.7 **BHPS 1991: Date current job began and number of employment/non-employment spells in year before interview by level and type of qualification held[a]**

Continuity of employment	Higher academic	Higher VQ	All highly qualified	Less qualified	All women	
	%	%	%	%	Freq	%
Date current job began						
Over one year ago	62.8	69.4	66.6	71.8	1566	70.4
Less than one year ago	37.2	30.6	33.4	28.2	657	29.6
Base = 100%	242	320	562	1661	2223	
*Number of employers***						
None	9.1	17.2	13.8	29.5	915	26.1
One	81.5	70.7	75.3	61.9	2269	64.8
Two	8.2	9.8	9.2	7.1	265	7.6
Three or more	0.0	1.9	1.1	1.1	39	1.1
Missing/DK	0.9	0.5	0.6	0.4	15	0.4
*Number of employment spells***						
None	9.1	17.2	13.8	29.4	914	26.1
One	72.1	65.3	68.3	59.2	2140	61.1
Two	16.3	15.1	15.6	9.6	382	10.9
Three or more	1.3	1.9	1.7	1.4	52	1.5
Missing/DK	0.9	0.5	0.6	0.4	15	0.4
Number of unemployment spells						
None	91.5	95.3	93.8	92.9	3260	93.1
One	6.0	3.5	5.9	6.2	206	5.9
Two or more	1.6	0.7	1.2	0.5	23	0.7
Missing/DK	0.9	0.5	0.6	0.4	15	0.4
*Number of inactive spells***						
None	73.7	76.0	75.2	63.3	2304	65.8
One	22.3	23.0	22.8	34.9	1131	32.3
Two or more	2.8	0.5	1.5	1.5	52	1.5
Missing/DK	0.9	0.5	0.6	0.4	15	0.4
Base[b] = 100%	319	430	749	2354	3503	

a   *Women aged 20 - 59 years.*

b   *Column percentages calculated on the base figures shown.*

**   *Sig. <.001.*

Table 6.8   BHPS 1991: Whether currently in paid employment by employment one year before interview and level and type of qualification held[a]

Current employment status	Employment one year before interview		All Women	
	In employment	Not in employment		
	%	%	Freq	%
*All women***				
In employment	91.5	15.4	2326	66.9
Not in employment[b]	8.4	84.6	1152	33.1
Base = 100%	2351	1127	3478	
*All highly qualified***				
In employment	94.0	28.8	597	80.5
Not in employment	6.0	71.2	145	19.5
Base = 100%	588	154	742	
*Academic qualifications***				
In employment	93.6	46.0	264	83.9
Not in employment	6.4	54.0	50	16.1
Base = 100%	251	63	314	
*Vocational qualification***				
In employment	94.4	16.7	333	78.0
Not in employment	5.6	83.3	94	22.0
Base = 100%	337	90	427	
*Less qualified***				
In employment	90.8	13.3	1729	63.2
Not in employment	9.2	86.7	1007	36.8
Base[c] = 100%	1763	973	2736	

a   Women aged 20 - 59 years.

b   Not in employment includes unemployed and economically inactive.

c   Column percentages calculated on the base figures shown.

**   Sig <.001.

It is also noticeable that for all women who were in paid employment at the time of interview their spouse/partner was more likely to have been in paid employment a year before interview than the spouse/partners of women who were not in employment at the time of interview, a relationship which holds regardless of the level of qualification held by the woman.

Table 6.9   BHPS 1991: Spouse's employment characteristics by level and type of qualification held by women in married or cohabiting couples

Spouse's employment characteristics	Qualification held				All women	
	Higher academic	Higher VQ	All highly qualified	Less qualified		
	%	%	%	%	Freq	%
Whether in current paid employment						
No	7.9	11.1	9.8	15.6	370	14.4
Yes	92.1	88.6	90.2	84.4	2220	85.6
Base = 100%	214	325	539	2031	2570	
Occupation						
Manager/professional	75.1	51.5	61.0	31.3	777	38.0
Clerical/craft	13.5	25.7	20.8	34.6	644	31.5
Services/sales	7.0	8.5	7.8	9.6	188	9.2
Plant/other	4.3	14.7	10.4	24.4	434	21.3
Base = 100%	185	272	457	1586	2043	
Usual hours worked per week						
<16 hours	3.3	0.8	1.7	0.9	22	1.1
16-29 hours	2.7	1.9	2.2	1.7	36	1.1
30-30 hours	51.1	45.2	47.6	44.9	906	45.5
40+ hours	43.4	52.1	48.5	52.2	1027	51.6
Base = 100%	182	261	443	1548	1991	
Monthly gross earnings						
<542	5.8	2.2	3.8	4.8	74	4.6
542-875	6.5	11.2	9.3	20.6	289	17.9
876-1321	19.5	30.5	26.1	35.7	539	33.5
1321 thru hi	67.5	56.1	60.8	38.9	707	44.0
Base = 100%	154	223	377	1232	1609	
Whether in employment one year before interview						
No	4.1	9.8	7.5	10.1	219	9.6
Yes	95.9	90.2	92.5	89.8	1868	90.4
Base = 100%	195	295	490	1797	2287	

a   Column percentages calculated on the base figures shown.

b   Note that the base n varies due to the amount of available information about the spouse for each.

employment characteristic

Sig. <.01.

Table 6.10 BHPS 1991: Spouse's employment characteristics by current employment and level and type of qualification held by women in married or cohabiting couples

Spouse's employment characteristics	In employment			Not in employment		All women	
	Higher academic	Higher VQ	Less qualified	All highly qualified	Less qualified		
	%	%	%	%	%	Freq	%
Whether in current paid employment							
No	7.2	7.6	9.0	20.4	28.8	370	14.4
Yes	92.8	92.4	91.1	80.6	71.2	2200	85.6
Base = 100%	181	250	1350	108	681	2570	
Occupation							
Manager/professional	74.4	52.8	30.5	56.3	33.6	777	38.0
Clerical/craft	13.8	24.8	34.9	23.8	33.9	644	31.5
Services/sales	7.5	7.8	10.0	7.5	8.6	188	9.2
Plant/other	5.0	14.2	24.7	11.3	23.6	434	21.3
Base = 100%	160	218	1146	80	440	2043	
Usual hours worked per week							
<16 hours	3.2	0.0	0.8	3.8	1.2	22	1.1
16-29 hours	1.9	1.9	1.5	3.8	2.3	36	1.8
30-30 hours	52.6	45.7	46.4	43.0	40.9	906	45.4
40+ hours	42.3	52.9	51.3	49.4	55.6	1027	51.6
Base = 100%	156	208	1120	79	428	1991	
Monthly gross earnings							
<542	6.8	2.2	4.3	1.5	6.0	74	4.6
542-875	6.8	11.2	20.7	9.2	20.5	289	17.9
876-1321	22.6	30.9	37.1	21.5	31.9	539	33.5
1321 thru hi	63.9	55.6	37.9	67.7	41.6	708	44.0
Base = 100%	133	178	900	65	332	1609	
Whether in employment one year before interview							
No	3.7	5.7	5.2	17.5	20.4	219	9.6
Yes	96.3	94.3	94.9	82.5	70.6	2068	90.4
Base = 100%	164	228	1203	97	594	2287	

a Column percentages calculated on the base figures shown.

b Note that the base n varies due to the amount of available information about the spouse for each
employment characteristic.

Sg. <.001.

Job satisfaction and reasons for working

All respondents in paid employment at the time of interview were asked to rank how satisfied or dissatisfied they were with aspects of their current job on a seven point scale where one equalled not satisfied at all; seven equalled completely satisfied and four equalled neither satisfied nor dissatisfied[10]. Seven items were specified for employees as follows:

> *Promotion prospects*
>
> *The total pay, including any overtime or bonuses*
>
> *Relations with your supervisor or manager*
>
> *Your job security*
>
> *Being able to use your own initiative*
>
> *The actual work itself*
>
> *The hours you work.*

The self-employed were asked to rank the following five items using the same seven point scale:

> *The total pay, including any overtime or bonuses*
>
> *Your job security*
>
> *Being able to use your own initiative*
>
> *The actual work itself*
>
> *The hours you work.*

Both employees and the self-employed were then asked

> *'All things considered, how satisfied or dissatisfied are you with your present job overall using the same 1-7 scale?'.*

For the self-employed there were no statistically significant differences according to level or type of qualification held on any of the specified items or on overall job satisfaction. For employees however there were marked differences between the highly qualified and the less qualified on all specified items and on overall job satisfaction. Table 6.11 sets out the distribution for each item according to the level and type of qualification held for all women employees. On overall job satisfaction highly qualified women were less likely than less qualified women to say they were completely satisfied with their current job. Only 27% (n=149) of highly qualified women gave this response compared to 42% (n=690) of less qualified women. The type of higher qualification held also affected the ranking of overall job satisfaction with the vocationally qualified being more likely than those with academic qualifications to say they were completely satisfied with their current job. Of those with higher academic qualifications, 15% (n=37) said they were completely satisfied with their current job overall compared to 35% (n=112) of those with higher vocational qualifications. Further, if we look at the combined percentages for rankings six and seven on the scale the percentage of those with higher vocational qualifications in these categories is virtually the same as for less qualified women. The total percentage of the higher vocationally qualified falling in these two ranking categories was 67% (n=215), compared to 66% (n=1097) of the less qualified, and 50% (n=120) of the higher academically qualified. This suggests that while highly qualified women may have a greater commitment to paid employment, their expectations may also be higher in terms of what constitutes a satisfying job, particularly for those with academic qualifications. A similar pattern is found on all the specified aspects of the current job, with the less qualified consistently ranking their satisfaction on each item higher than the highly qualified.

The number of hours worked by women also affected women's overall satisfaction with their current job. Women working part-time were more likely than full-time workers to say they were completely satisfied with their job, 47% and 32% respectively. When we control for the level of qualification held, this relationship holds across all levels of qualification. Higher qualified women were, however, less likely than less qualified women to say they were completely satisfied, regardless of the number of hours worked.

Gender is a further element to be considered. As has been documented elsewhere, women tend to report higher levels of overall job satisfaction than men. This pattern is confirmed in the BHPS data where 39% (n=970) of women employees were completely satisfied with their current job compared to 25% (n=675) of male employees. When we compare women and men with similar levels of qualification a slightly different pattern emerges. For those holding higher academic qualifications there are no gender differences in job satisfaction with only 15% reporting themselves completely satisfied in each case. Where vocational qualifications or less qualifications are held, gender is significant. Of women with higher vocational qualifications, 35% (n=112) were completely satisfied compared with 22% (n=86) of similarly qualified men. Of less qualified women, 42% (n=690) were completely satisfied compared to 27% (n=463) of less qualified men.

Table 6.12 gives the mean score of each item according to the level and type of qualification held for male and female employees only. A t-test between the mean scores for all highly qualified women and less qualified women showed statistically significant differences in the means for overall job satisfaction, promotion prospects, total pay and the actual work itself.

Table 6.11 BHPS 1991: Job satisfaction by level and type of qualification held - women employees only[a]

Satisfaction	Qualification				All women	
	Higher academic	Higher VQ	All highly qualified	Less qualified		
	%	%	%	%	Freq	%
*Overall***						
Not satisfied at all	2.5	1.9	2.2	3.2	65	2.9
	3.7	0.6	2.0	1.4	35	1.6
	9.1	4.1	6.3	2.4	75	3.4
Neither sat/dissatisfied	11.6	8.1	9.6	11.0	236	10.6
	23.1	17.8	20.1	15.8	376	16.9
	34.3	32.2	33.0	24.5	592	26.6
Completely satisfied	15.3	35.0	26.6	41.5	840	37.8
Doesn't apply	0.0	0.3	0.2	0.2	4	0.2
*Promotion prospects***						
Not satisfied at all	14.9	10.3	12.3	14.9	316	14.2
	5.8	5.0	5.4	3.8	93	4.2
	7.4	6.9	7.0	4.5	114	5.1
Neither sat/dissatisfied	26.0	28.1	27.2	26.7	597	26.8
	17.4	9.7	13.0	7.2	192	8.6
	12.0	10.3	11.0	6.0	161	7.3
Completely satisfied	11.6	19.1	15.8	22.5	463	20.8
Doesn't apply	5.4	10.3	8.2	14.4	286	12.9
*Total pay***						
Not satisfied at all	11.2	10.0	10.4	11.7	253	11.4
	7.0	4.4	5.5	4.4	104	4.7
	13.6	12.8	13.2	7.7	201	9.0
Neither sat/dissatisfied	17.8	20.3	19.1	21.9	471	21.2
	21.9	17.2	19.2	13.4	331	14.9
	16.5	14.4	15.3	12.5	293	13.2
Completely satisfied	12.8	20.3	17.0	28.3	564	25.4
Doesn't apply	0.0	0.6	0.3	0.2	5	0.2
*Relations with supervisor***						
Not satisfied at all	4.6	2.8	3.6	3.0	71	3.2
	2.5	1.6	1.9	1.7	40	1.8
	5.0	5.6	5.3	2.4	70	3.1
Neither sat/dissatisfied	12.4	11.3	11.6	12.0	265	11.9
	17.4	9.1	12.6	10.6	246	11.1
	22.0	20.9	21.5	15.5	378	17.0
Completely satisfied	35.3	47.8	42.5	53.1	1119	50.4
Doesn't apply	0.8	1.3	1.0	1.6	32	1.4

Continued on next page

Table 6.11 BHPS 1991: Job satisfaction by level and type of qualification held - women employees only[a] (continued)

Satisfaction	Qualification				All women	
	Higher academic	Higher VQ	All highly qualified	Less qualified		
	%	%	%	%	Freq	%
*Job security***						
Not satisfied at all	5.8	7.8	6.9	7.6	165	7.4
	4.1	2.2	3.8	3.1	68	3.0
	7.0	5.9	6.4	3.8	100	4.5
Neither sat/dissatisfied	14.9	11.9	13.1	15.4	329	14.8
	15.3	14.7	14.9	10.5	258	11.6
	22.3	17.2	19.4	13.7	337	15.2
Completely satisfied	28.5	39.4	34.8	44.6	935	42.1
Doesn't apply	1.7	1.3	1.4	1.3	30	1.4
*Being able to use own initiative***						
Not satisfied at all	3.7	1.9	2.7	3.9	79	3.6
	2.1	0.6	1.3	1.4	31	1.4
	6.2	3.8	4.8	2.3	65	2.9
Neither sat/dissatisfied	9.1	6.6	7.7	10.5	217	9.8
	17.4	11.9	14.1	10.7	257	11.6
	23.6	27.2	25.6	17.1	428	19.3
Completely satisfied	37.6	47.2	43.1	53.4	1129	50.8
Doesn't apply	0.4	0.6	0.6	0.7	15	0.7
*Actual work itself***						
Not satisfied at all	4.1	1.3	2.5	3.6	74	3.3
	3.7	0.6	2.0	1.3	32	1.5
	5.8	1.3	3.1	2.7	61	2.8
Neither sat/dissatisfied	8.3	8.1	8.2	14.0	279	12.6
	21.5	13.1	16.7	12.2	296	13.3
	29.3	29.4	29.4	18.0	464	20.9
Completely satisfied	27.7	45.9	38.0	48.3	1015	45.7
*Hours worked***						
Not satisfied at all	5.4	4.7	5.1	3.7	90	4.0
	7.0	3.8	5.2	1.7	57	2.5
	11.6	6.9	8.9	4.2	119	5.4
Neither sat/dissatisfied	15.7	14.4	15.0	16.0	350	15.7
	18.2	13.1	15.3	12.5	294	13.2
	20.2	16.9	18.2	15.1	352	15.9
Completely satisfied	21.5	40.3	32.3	46.7	956	43.0
Doesn't apply	0.0	0.3	0.2	0.2	6	0.2
Base = 100%	242	320	562	1660	2222	

** Sig. <.001.

a Column percentages calculated on the base figures shown.

Table 6.12   BHPS 1991: Mean scores for job satisfaction items according to level and type of qualification held - employees only

Job satisfaction	Higher academic	Higher VQ	Mean score All highly qualified	Less qualified	All
Women					
Overall satisfaction	5.13	5.74	5.48	5.73	5.67
Promotion prospects	3.90	3.97	3.94	3.72	3.77
Total pay	4.32	4.52	4.43	4.70	4.64
Relations with supervisor	5.41	5.71	5.58	5.79	5.74
Job security	5.06	5.29	5.19	5.33	5.30
Use of initiative	5.53	5.93	5.76	5.85	5.83
Work itself	5.37	6.03	5.75	5.76	5.76
Hours	4.80	5.37	5.13	5.63	5.50
Number of valid cases	242	320	562	1660	2222
Men					
Overall satisfaction	5.28	5.36	5.32	5.23	5.26
Promotion prospects	4.21	4.07	4.13	3.75	3.86
Total pay	4.58	4.67	4.63	4.14	4.28
Relations with supervisor	5.30	5.44	5.38	5.33	5.34
Job security	4.87	5.01	4.95	4.92	4.93
Use of initiative	5.78	5.95	5.88	5.78	5.81
Work itself	5.55	5.71	5.64	5.49	5.54
Hours	4.92	5.12	5.03	5.04	5.04
Number of valid cases	321	384	705	1744	2449

Important aspects of jobs

In addition to ranking their satisfaction with their current job, respondents who were in paid employment, unemployed at the time of interview or who were inactive, but said they would like to have some paid employment even if only for a few hours per week, were asked about their motivations for wanting employment. They were asked to specify the two most important aspects of a job and the two most important reasons for wanting a job from a listing of seven different items. For the most important aspects of a job these included;

Promotion prospects

The total pay, including any overtime or bonuses

Relations with your supervisor or manager

Your job security

Being able to use your own initiative

The actual work itself

The hours you work.

Other aspect (specify)

The reasons for wanting a job included;

Working is the normal thing to do

To pay for essentials such as food, mortgage, rent and bills.

To earn money to buy extras

To earn money of my own

For the company of other people

Enjoy working

To follow my career

Other reason (specify)

Table 6.13 suggests that for the most important aspect of a job, the actual work itself was the aspect cited most often by 34% of women (n=1027). The highly qualified were more likely than the less qualified to specify this as the most important aspect of a job with 56% (n=377) of the highly qualified compared to 28% (n=650) of less qualified women citing this. Again there was a difference within the highly qualified group according to the type of qualification held with the academically qualified being most likely to specify the actual work as the most important aspect of a job. It is interesting to note that although the higher academically qualified women clearly felt that the actual work is the most important aspect of a job, those who were in employment expressed the least satisfaction with this aspect of their current job in the job satisfaction

rankings (see Table 6.11). This offers some confirmation for the suggestion that academically qualified women may have higher expectations of employment which are not always met by the jobs they hold. Although promotion prospects, total pay, being able to use their own initiative and hours worked did not emerge as being the most important aspects of jobs for highly qualified women, these items were specified more or less evenly across the distribution for the second most important aspect of a job. Being able to use their own initiative was the item most often specified by highly qualified women after the actual work itself. Academically qualified women were more likely than either the vocationally qualified or the less qualified to give total pay as the second most important aspect of a job. Of the higher academically qualified, 25% (n=75) gave this

Table 6.13   BHPS 1991: Most important aspects of a job by level and type of qualification[a]

	Qualification				All women	
Aspect of job	Higher academic	Higher VQ	All highly qualified	Less qualified		
	%	%	%	%	Freq	%
*Most important aspect***						
Promotion prospects	2.4	1.5	1.9	2.2	65	2.1
Total pay	7.0	8.1	7.6	15.3	410	13.6
Good relations manager	2.8	6.9	5.1	10.6	282	9.4
Job security	5.8	13.8	10.3	25.6	668	22.2
Using initiative	14.2	8.3	10.9	8.3	268	8.9
Actual work	60.3	52.7	56.1	27.8	1027	34.3
Hours worked	3.9	5.7	7.5	8.2	225	7.5
Other	3.7	2.9	3.3	1.8	63	2.1
Missing	-	-	-	-	4	-
*2nd most important aspect***						
Promotion prospects	5.8	4.8	5.2	3.7	121	4.0
Total pay	18.6	18.2	18.4	22.7	653	21.7
Good relations manager	14.8	15.6	15.3	16.8	494	16.5
Job security	6.5	16.7	12.2	14.1	411	13.7
Using initiative	25.4	16.9	20.6	12.1	421	14.0
Actual work	16.9	16.6	16.7	18.1	535	17.8
Hours worked	5.7	8.6	7.4	10.8	301	10.0
Other	6.3	2.6	4.2	1.6	66	2.2
Missing	-	-	-	-	9	-
Base = 100%	297	374	671	2340	3011	

a   *Column percentages calculated on the base figures shown.*

**   *Sig. <.001.*

58

response compared to 17% (n=63) of the vocationally qualified and 12% (n=283) of less qualified women.

In Table 6.14 we found that the most important reason for wanting a job given by women, was to pay for essentials such as food, housing costs and bills. Overall 41% (n=1230) of women gave this as the most important reason although those with less qualifications were more likely to give this response than highly qualified women. Of the less qualified 43% (n=1011) gave this as the most important reason compared to 33% (n=219) of the highly qualified. Less qualified women were also more likely than the higher qualified to give other financial reasons for wanting a job including to earn money for extras and to earn money for themselves. In contrast the highly qualified were more likely than the less qualified to give intrinsic reasons for wanting a job including because they enjoyed working, 22% (n=149) and to follow their career, 17% (n=113). The type of higher qualification held affected the responses once again with higher percentages of the higher academically qualified giving these intrinsic responses than the vocationally qualified.

Table 6.14   BHPS 1991: Most important reasons for wanting a job by level and type of qualification[a]

Aspect of job	Higher academic	Higher VQ	All highly qualified	Less qualified	All women	
	%	%	%	%	Freq	%
*Most important aspect***						
Normal thing to do	2.0	3.8	3.0	2.2	70	2.3
Essential for food, bills, etc.	30.1	34.6	32.6	43.2	1230	40.9
Money for extras	4.6	10.2	7.7	17.2	453	15.1
Earn money for self	7.2	11.8	9.8	14.1	396	13.2
For people's company	2.8	3.9	3.4	6.2	168	5.6
Enjoy working	26.4	18.8	22.2	11.4	416	13.8
Follow career	20.2	14.3	16.9	3.8	202	6.7
Other	6.7	2.6	4.4	1.9	75	2.5
*2nd most important reason***						
Normal thing to do	2.3	3.3	2.9	3.9	110	3.7
Essential for food, bills, etc.	16.3	10.1	12.8	11.6	357	11.9
Money for extras	6.8	14.1	10.9	23.6	623	20.8
Earn money for self	16.7	15.5	16.0	18.6	540	18.0
For people's company	12.0	11.5	11.7	15.9	448	14.9
Enjoy working	23.7	22.8	23.2	19.5	610	20.4
Follow career	19.2	20.2	19.7	5.2	253	8.4
Other	2.9	2.5	2.7	1.7	57	1.9
Missing	-	-	-	-	34	-
Base = 100%	297	374	671	2340	3011	

a   *Column percentages calculated on the base figures shown.*

**   *Sig. <.001.*

Family responsibilities and childcare

All respondents of working age were asked if family responsibilities had affected their employment in the past year and if so to specify the type of responsibility. Respondents were asked if in the past year family responsibilities had *prevented* them from looking for a job; from accepting a full-time job they were offered or from changing jobs; and if family responsibilities had *required* them to change jobs; to leave paid employment or to work fewer hours. Table 6.15 gives the distributions on each item according to the level and type of qualification held. The only items where there was a statistically significant relationship with the level of qualifications held were the cases where family responsibilities had prevented the respondent looking for a job and with the type of responsibility which had affected their employment. Overall the highly qualified were less likely to say they had been prevented from looking for a job because of family responsibilities than less qualified women. Of the highly qualified 12% (n=92) gave this response compared to 20% (n=542) of less qualified women. Childcare was the reason mentioned by the majority of all women reporting some form of employment constraint due to family responsibilities over the past year with 78% (n=671) citing childcare responsibilities of some type[11]. The most marked difference was between women with higher academic qualifications and less qualified women. Sixty nine percent (n=50) of the higher academically qualified and 79% (n=548) of the less qualified cited childcare as the reason their employment had been constrained. However, women with higher academic qualifications were more likely than the less qualified to give 'other' reasons for their employment being constrained. Of the highly qualified 19% (n=14) gave an 'other' reason compared to 6% (n=44) of the less qualified. As those with higher academic qualifications were less likely to have dependent children than less qualified women it might be expected that fewer would give childcare as the reason their employment had been constrained. However, the data suggest that other family responsibilities may play a greater part in constraining the employment of highly qualified women than for less qualified women.

While the level of qualification has some effect on whether women say their employment has been constrained over the past year, when we control for current employment status it is clear that the type of constraint reported also depends upon whether the respondent had been employed in the past year and is currently employed. Table 6.16 suggests that those who were not in employment at the time of interview were more likely than the employed to say they had been prevented from looking for a job by family responsibilities regardless of the level or type of qualification held. Similarly those in current employment were more likely to say they had been prevented from changing jobs than those not in employment while a higher percentage of those not in employment said they had been required to leave paid employment due to family responsibilities. Further those not in current employment were more likely to give childcare responsibilities as the reason their employment had been constrained than those currently employed.

Table 6.15 BHPS 1991: Family responsibilities affecting employment in past year by level and type of qualification - women aged 20-59 years[a]

Family responsibility	Higher academic	Higher VQ	All highly qualified	Less qualified	All women	
	%	%	%	%	Freq	%
Prevented looking for job**						
Yes	12.9	11.9	12.3	19.7	633	18.1
No	86.5	87.4	87.0	79.2	2831	80.8
Missing/DK	0.6	0.7	0.7	1.2	39	1.1
Prevented accepting full-time job						
Yes	5.6	7.9	7.0	8.6	289	8.3
No	93.4	90.9	92.1	90.1	3170	90.5
Missing/DK	0.6	1.2	0.9	1.3	43	1.2
Prevented changing jobs						
Yes	9.4	7.0	8.1	6.1	230	6.6
No	90.0	91.9	91.1	92.5	3229	92.2
Missing/DK	0.3	1.2	0.8	1.4	45	1.3
Required job change						
Yes	3.1	3.0	3.1	1.8	74	2.1
No	95.6	95.6	95.7	96.8	3382	96.6
Missing/DK	0.9	1.4	1.2	1.4	47	1.3
Required leave paid employment						
Yes	3.8	4.4	4.1	4.2	146	4.2
No	95.3	94.2	94.8	94.4	3311	94.5
Missing/DK	0.9	1.4	1.2	1.3	46	1.3
Required working fewer hours						
Yes	6.9	4.9	5.8	4.6	170	4.8
No	92.2	93.7	93.1	94.0	3287	93.8
Missing/DK	0.6	1.4	1.0	1.4	46	1.3
Base = 100%	319	430	749	2754	3503	
Responsibility affecting employment*						
Childcare	69.4	75.5	72.8	79.4	671	78.1
Other family care	11.1	11.2	11.5	14.2	118	13.7
Other	19.4	13.3	15.7	6.4	71	8.2
Base = 100%	72	98	170	690	860	

a   *Column percentages calculated on the base figures shown.*

*   *Sg. <.01.*

** *Sig. <.001.*

61

Table 6.16 BHPS 1991: Family responsibilities affecting employment by current employment and qualification held[b]

Family responsibility	In employment			Not in employment		All women	
	Higher academic	Higher VQ	Less qualified	All highly qualified	Less qualified		
	%	%	%	%	%	Freq	%
*Prevented looking for job***							
Yes	7.7	6.1	8.0	37.3	40.8	633	18.1
No	91.6	93.0	90.7	61.9	58.1	2831	80.8
Missing/DK	0.4	0.9	1.3	0.7	1.0	39	1.1
Prevented accepting full-time job							
Yes	5.1	8.2	7.4	7.5	10.7	289	8.3
No	94.1	90.6	91.2	91.0	88.1	3170	90.5
Missing/DK	0.4	1.5	1.4	0.7	1.3	43	1.2
*Prevented changing jobs***							
Yes	10.3	7.9	7.8	3.5	3.1	230	6.6
No	89.7	90.9	90.7	94.8	95.6	3229	92.2
Missing/DK	0.0	1.5	1.5	0.7	1.3	45	1.3
Required job change							
Yes	3.7	3.2	2.0	2.2	1.5	74	2.1
No	95.6	95.6	96.6	96.3	97.2	3382	96.6
Missing/DK	0.7	1.5	1.4	1.5	1.3	47	1.3
*Required leave paid job***							
Yes	2.2	2.6	1.9	11.9	8.4	146	4.2
No	97.1	95.9	96.7	87.3	90.3	3311	94.5
Missing/DK	0.7	1.8	1.4	0.7	1.3	46	1.3
Required fewer working hours							
Yes	7.7	5.0	5.4	4.5	3.1	170	4.8
No	91.9	93.6	93.2	94.0	95.5	3287	93.8
Missing/DK	0.4	1.8	1.4	0.7	1.4	46	1.3
Base = 100%	273	342	1777	134	977	3503	
*Responsibility affecting employment***							
Childcare	63.0	71.4	75.1	83.0	82.2	671	78.1
Other family care	13.0	11.1	13.0	11.3	15.1	118	13.7
Other	25.9	17.5	11.6	3.8	2.7	71	8.2
Base[a] = 100%	54	63	285	53	405	860	

a Column percentages calculated on the base figures shown.

b Women aged 20-59 years.

** Sig. <.001.

For women with dependent children combining paid employment and caring for children is a central issue. The availability of suitable childcare facilities and the cost of childcare are factors which influence women's decisions about taking on paid employment and the terms on which they are able to do so. In the BHPS survey all women who were in current employment and who had at least one dependent child aged twelve years or under were asked a series of questions regarding the type of childcare used while they were at work, whether this care was free or paid for, who paid for childcare which was not free and who was considered to be responsible for children when they were ill. These 752 women were asked to mention up to three types of childcare used. The only statistically significant relationship between the type of childcare used and level and type of qualification held was on the first mentioned type of childcare used. In Table 6.17 we find that less qualified women were more likely than highly qualified women to work while the children were at school or to say their spouse/partner cared for the children when they were working. In addition, highly qualified women were more likely to use a formal type of childcare such as a workplace nursery, a day nursery, a nanny/mothers help or a

childminder than less qualified women. Of highly qualified women 28% (n=24) used one of these types of care compared to 10% (n=55) of less qualified women. However there was little difference where an informal type of care provided by a relative or friend was used although those women with higher academic qualifications were least likely to rely on this type of informal care.

The type of childcare used may be determined in some instances by the hours worked and the woman's level of earnings with the highly qualified tending to work longer hours and to have higher earnings which enable the purchase of childcare. This is confirmed in the data, shown in Table 6.18, where 53% (n=60) of highly qualified women said they paid for childcare compared to 33% (n=97) of less qualified women. The type of higher qualification also affected whether childcare was free or paid for, with a higher percentage of the higher academically qualified paying for childcare than the higher vocationally qualified. Although there was a statistically significant relationship between whether childcare was free or paid for with the level and type of qualification held, no such relationships existed for the weekly cost of childcare or who paid for

Table 6.17   BHPS 1991: Type of childcare used[b] for children aged 12 years or under - women in current employment only

Type of childcare used	Higher academic	Higher VQ	All highly qualified	Less qualified	All women	
	%	%	%	%	Freq	%
Work when at school	25.9	24.7	25.2	29.9	216	28.8
Look after themselves	3.9	3.8	3.8	3.7	28	3.8
Work from home	6.3	4.6	5.3	6.0	44	5.9
Spouse/partner cares	10.1	19.1	15.4	25.2	172	22.9
Nanny/mother's help	6.6	0.9	3.2	1.3	13	1.8
Workplace nursery	2.4	1.1	1.6	=	3	0.4
Day nursery	8.4	3.8	5.7	3.0	27	3.6
Childminder	14.6	13.4	13.9	5.3	55	7.3
Relative	12.1	19.3	16.4	16.3	123	16.3
Friend/neighbour	1.6	3.5	2.7	3.1	23	3.0
Other	5.1	2.7	3.7	3.1	25	3.3
Missing	3.0	3.1	3.1	3.1	22	3.1
Base[a] = 100%	72	104	176	575	751	

a   Column percentages calculated on base figures shown.

b   First mentioned type of care used only.

63

childcare. However, a higher percentage of highly qualified women paid over £30 per week for childcare when compared to less qualified women. In addition highly qualified women were more likely to say they shared the cost of childcare with their partner, compared to less qualified women who tended to say that they paid for all of the childcare out of their own wage. The data therefore suggest that the critical factor for less qualified women is whether free childcare is available or not.

The final question asked of working women with children aged twelve or under was who cared for children when they were ill. Table 6.18 shows no marked differences in who cared for children when they were ill according to the level and type of

Table 6.18   BHPS 1991: Childcare costs and caring for ill children by level and type of qualification - women in current employment with dependent children aged 12 years or under

Childcare payment	Higher academic	Higher VQ	All highly qualified	Less qualified	All women	
	%	%	%	%	Freq	%
*Whether childcare free or paid***						
Childcare free	38.3	50.0	45.2	65.3	243	59.6
Childcare paid	59.6	48.5	53.0	33.0	157	38.5
Missing/DK	2.1	1.5	1.8	1.7	7	1.8
Base = 100%	47	66	113	294	407	
Weekly cost of childcare						
<£10	13.8	21.2	19.2	27.2	40	24.4
£11-20	6.9	18.2	12.0	19.4	28	16.7
£21-30	13.8	24.2	18.6	16.5	28	17.1
over £30	58.6	30.3	43.0	26.2	54	32.5
Missing/DK	10.3	6.1	7.1	10.7	15	9.2
Who pays for childcare						
All from own wage	44.8	42.4	44.6	65.0	95	57.8
Most from own wage	6.9	0.0	3.0	0.0	2	1.1
Share costs spouse/partner	31.0	45.5	37.9	23.3	48	29.1
Most by spouse/partner	0.0	3.0	1.8	3.9	5	2.9
All by spouse/partner	10.3	6.1	7.5	1.0	5	3.3
Other	3.4	0.0	1.9	1.0	2	1.3
Missing/DK	3.4	3.0	3.3	4.9	8	4.6
Base = 100%	29	33	62	103	165	
Who cares for ill children						
Respondent	68.1	64.4	65.2	67.0	500	66.6
Spouse/partner	16.7	8.7	11.8	10.4	81	10.8
Mother's help/nanny	1.4	1.0	1.2	1.7	13	1.7
Relative	5.6	12.5	9.5	11.0	80	10.6
Friend/neighbour	2.8	2.9	2.6	2.1	16	2.2
Other	4.2	7.7	6.2	3.8	33	4.4
Missing/DK	2.8	3.8	3.5	3.8	28	3.7
Base[a] = 100%	72	104	177	575	752	

a   Column percentages calculated from base figures shown.

**   Sig. <.001.

qualification held by the woman. The majority of all women with children in this age group said they looked after ill children. Overall 67% (n=500) of women said they cared for ill children, 11% (n=81) said their spouse/partner provided care and 11% (n=80) said a relative provided care in these circumstances.

Domestic division of labour

All married or cohabiting respondents were asked a series of questions on the domestic division of labour to establish who carried out various household chores including shopping, cooking, cleaning, washing/ironing and looking after children aged twelve years or under. From Table 6.19 we see that while the level and type of qualification held was significant for some tasks, it is the employment status of the woman in combination with her qualifications which has the most marked effect on which couple member does various tasks. On all items except shopping women who were not in employment at the time of interview were more likely to say they did the task involved regardless of the level of their qualifications (see Table 6.20). On all the specified tasks women with higher academic qualifications who were in employment were least likely to say they did each task 'mostly themselves' and more likely to say they shared the task with their partner than other employed women. In the case of 'cleaning' 14% of employed higher academically qualified women said that someone other than themselves or their partner did the cleaning, which suggests that these mainly professional women are buying in this labour from outside the home. The difference between employed and non-employed women is particularly striking with regard to who looks after children; 46% (n=28) of higher or academically qualified women who were in employment said they looked after children mostly themselves compared to 89% (n=55) of highly qualified women who were not in employment. It seems likely therefore that it is the pressure on time experienced by women combining work and family commitments rather than the level of qualifications *per se* which affects who does various household chores and caring activities within the home. That highly qualified women and particularly academically qualified women tend to be in full-time jobs therefore has a greater affect on the domestic division of labour than in other couple households.

Attitudes to the family and women's employment

In the BHPS survey respondents were asked a series of questions on their attitudes towards family responsibilities and women's employment. Respondents were asked to say how strongly they agreed or disagreed with a set of statements ranked on a five point scale. The statements were:

> A pre-school child is likely to suffer if his or her mother works.
>
> All in all, family life suffers when the woman has a full-time job.
>
> A woman and her family would all be happier if she goes out to work.
>
> Both the husband and wife should contribute to the household income.
>
> Having a full-time job is the best way for a woman to be an independent person.
>
> A husband's job is to earn money; a wife's job is to look after the home and family.
>
> Children need a father to be as closely involved in their upbringing as the mother.
>
> Employers should make special arrangements to help mothers combine jobs and childcare.
>
> A single parent can bring up children as well as a couple.

Table 6.21 suggests that overall women with higher qualifications had less traditional attitudes than less qualified women[12]. When we create a four item scale on the attitudinal items from 'traditional' to 'modern' the majority of all women, 65% (n=2264) are found in the 'mixed modern' while 18% (n=614) are in the 'mixed traditional category' and 15% (n=539) in the 'modern' category. The most marked differences between those with higher qualifications and those with less qualifications are the percentages with 'modern' attitudes, 23% (n=170) of highly qualified women were in this category compared to 14% (n=369) of less qualified women. However whether the woman was in paid employment at the time of interview also had an affect on the attitudes held (see Table 6.22). As might be expected highly qualified women, and those with academic qualifications in particular, who were in paid employment were more likely to hold 'modern' attitudes than less qualified women in employment. Women who were not in employment held more traditional attitudes overall and it is interesting to note that the non-employed highly qualified women held the most traditional attitudes when compared to all other groups, including the less qualified employed and non-employed women. Of the highly qualified women not in employment, 30% (n=40)

Table 6.19   BHPS 1991: Who does household chores by level and type of qualification held - married/cohabiting women[b]

Domestic task	Qualification				All women	
	Higher academic	Higher VQ	All highly qualified	Less qualified		
	%	%	%	%	Freq	%
Who does shopping						
Mostly self	51.9	56.6	54.6	56.2	1447	55.8
Mostly partner	9.7	7.6	8.4	7.3	194	7.5
Shared	37.0	34.9	35.8	34.8	907	35.0
Other	0.0	0.3	0.2	0.9	20	0.8
Missing/DK	1.4	0.6	0.9	0.9	24	0.9
Who does cooking						
Mostly self	68.5	70.0	69.4	73.4	1881	72.6
Mostly partner	5.1	5.5	5.3	6.0	151	5.8
Shared	24.5	23.5	23.9	19.1	521	20.1
Other	0.5	0.3	0.4	0.6	15	0.6
Missing/DK	1.4	0.6	0.9	0.9	24	0.9
*Who does cleaning**						
Mostly self	53.2	65.1	60.5	72.7	1818	70.1
Mostly partner	8.8	4.3	6.1	3.6	106	4.1
Shared	24.1	22.0	22.8	19.9	532	20.5
Other	12.5	7.3	9.4	2.9	110	4.2
Missing/DK	1.4	0.9	0.9	1.0	26	1.0
*Who does washing/ironing**						
Mostly self	65.7	80.7	74.9	86.4	2177	84.0
Mostly partner	3.2	1.5	2.2	1.5	42	1.6
Shared	24.1	14.7	18.4	9.0	284	10.9
Other	5.1	2.4	3.4	2.2	65	2.5
Missing/DK	1.9	0.6	0.9	0.9	25	1.0
Base[a] = 100%	216	327	543	2049	2592	
Who looks after children < 13 years						
Mainly respondent	58.1	71.4	65.9	70.3	779	69.4
Mainly partner	3.5	1.5	2.0	1.0	13	1.2
Joint with partner	43.9	26.3	29.9	26.2	302	26.9
Someone else	2.3	0.0	1.0	1.6	17	1.5
Missing/DK	2.3	0.8	0.9	0.9	11	1.0
Base[a] = 100%	86	133	219	903	1122	

a   *Column percentages calculated on the base figures shown.*

b   *Women aged 20-59 years.*

**   *Sig. <.001.*

Table 6.20   BHPS 1991: Who does domestic chores by current employment and level and type of qualification held[a] - married/cohabiting women[b]

Domestic task	In employment			Not in employment		All married women	
	Higher academic	Higher VQ	Less qualified	All highly qualified	Less qualified		
	%	%	%	%	%	Freq	%
Who does shopping							
Mostly self	51.4	58.3	57.8	50.9	53.1	1447	55.8
Mostly partner	9.4	5.6	7.3	12.7	7.3	194	7.5
Shared	38.1	34.5	33.4	34.5	37.6	907	35.0
Other	0.0	0.4	0.9	0.0	1.0	20	0.8
Missing/DK=	0.6	0.8	0.8	1.8	1.2	24	0.9
*Who does cooking**							
Mostly self	66.3	67.1	71.1	80.0	78.1	1881	72.6
Mostly partner	5.0	6.0	6.9	4.5	4.1	151	5.8
Shared	27.1	26.2	20.6	13.6	16.1	521	20.1
Other	0.6	0.0	0.6	0.9	0.7	15	0.6
Missing/DK=	0.6	0.8	0.8	1.8	1.2	24	0.9
*Who does cleaning***							
Mostly self	51.4	61.5	69.7	73.6	78.6	1818	70.1
Mostly partner	9.4	4.0	4.1	5.5	2.5	106	4.1
Shared	24.9	25.0	21.9	14.5	16.0	532	20.5
Other	13.8	8.3	3.4	4.5	1.9	110	4.2
Missing/DK=	0.6	1.2	1.0	1.8	1.2	26	1.0
*Who does washing/ironing***							
Mostly self	63.0	78.2	85.5	86.4	88.1	2177	84.0
Mostly partner	3.9	1.6	1.7	0.9	1.0	42	1.6
Shared	25.4	17.1	9.4	10.0	8.0	284	10.9
Other	6.1	2.4	2.6	0.9	1.6	65	2.5
Missing/DK=	1.1	0.8	0.8	1.8	1.2	24	1.0
Base = 100%	181	252	1361	110	688	2592	
*Who cares for children < 13 years***							
Mainly respondent	45.9	63.5	62.9	88.7	80.2	779	69.4
Mainly partner	4.9	1.0	1.7	1.6	0.0	13	1.2
Joint with partner	42.6	34.4	32.0	11.3	18.3	302	26.9
Someone else	3.3	0.0	1.9	0.0	1.3	17	1.5
Missing/DK	3.3	1.0	1.2	0.0	0.5	11	1.0
Base[a] = 100%	61	96	515	62	388	1122	

a   Column percentages calculated on base figures shown.

b   Women aged 20-59 years.

*   Sig. <.01.

**   Sig. <.001.

held mixed traditional attitudes compared to 11% (n=39) of those with vocational qualifications who were in employment and 9% (n=25) of those with academic qualifications who were in paid employment. In contrast 29% (n=79) of employed women with higher academic qualifications were in the 'modern' category compared to 11% (n=14) of non-employed highly qualified women.

For women, the number of hours worked might also be expected to be associated with their attitudes to employment and family life as women with less traditional attitudes may be more likely to work full time. When we look at attitudes held by level of qualification and control for whether women are in part-time or full-time employment there is no association between attitudes and qualifications for women working part-time. Where women are in full-time employment an association between attitudes and level of qualification is present with highly qualified women holding the least traditional attitudes. Of the highly qualified women in full-time employment 7% (n=32) held 'mixed traditional' attitudes compared to 12% (n=117) of the less qualified; 63% (n=277) had 'mixed modern' attitudes compared to 67% (n=654) of the less qualified and 30% (n=132) had 'modern' attitudes compared to 20% (n=197) of less qualified women.

When we compare the distributions of attitudes for men and women the majority of men were found in the 'mixed modern' category as were women. Men with higher qualifications were also more likely than less qualified men to hold 'modern' attitudes towards women's role in the home and employment. However overall men tended to be more traditional than women in their attitudes across all levels and types of qualification. Across all qualification levels men were about half as likely as women with similar qualifications to hold 'modern' attitudes. At the other end of the scale highly qualified men were twice as likely as their female counterparts to hold 'mixed traditional' attitudes. Where men were in employment their attitudes were significantly associated with the qualification held. The attitudes of non-employed men were not associated with their level of qualification.

Table 6.21 BHPS 1991: Attitudes to the family and employment by level and type of qualification[a]

Attitudes held	Qualification held				All	
	Higher academic	Higher VQ	All highly qualified	Less qualified		
	%	%	%	%	Freq	%
Women						
Traditional	0.6	0.9	0.8	0.9	29	0.8
Mixed traditional	11.9	15.2	13.9	18.9	614	17.8
Mixed modern	60.5	64.2	62.6	66.6	2264	65.7
Modern	27.0	19.7	22.7	13.7	539	15.6
Base = 100%	319	427	746	2700	3446	
Men						
Traditional	2.2	0.8	1.4	1.4	50	1.4
Mixed traditional	20.5	29.1	25.2	24.5	889	24.7
Mixed modern	63.0	61.2	62.0	66.6	2358	65.4
Modern	14.4	8.9	11.3	7.6	309	8.6
Base = 100%	427	523	950	2655	3605	

a   Column percentages calculated on the base figures shown.

Sig. <.001.

Table 6.22 BHPS 1991: Attitudes to the family and employment by level and type of qualification and current employment[a]

Attitudes held	In employment*			Not in employment*		All	
	Higher academic	Higher VQ	Less qualified	Highly qualified	Less qualified		
	%	%	%	%	%	Freq	%
Women							
Traditional	0.7	0.6	0.7	1.5	1.3	29	0.8
Mixed traditional	9.2	11.4	15.8	30.1	24.7	614	17.8
Mixed modern	61.2	65.4	67.5	57.1	64.8	2264	65.7
Modern	28.9	22.6	16.0	10.5	9.3	539	15.6
Base = 100%	273	341	1756	133	944	3446	
Men				ns	ns		
Traditional	2.5	0.7	1.2	1.0	1.8	50	1.4
Mixed traditional	20.6	28.6	23.8	27.4	26.7	889	24.7
Mixed modern	62.6	61.4	67.4	64.0	62.5	2358	65.4
Modern	14.3	9.4	7.6	7.5	9.1	309	8.6
Base = 100%	384	460	2072	106	583	3605	

a   Column percentages calculated on the base figures shown.

*   Sig. <.001.

ns Not significant.

Footnotes to Section 6

1. Those not in employment include the unemployed and the economically inactive.

2. Earnings quartiles calculated from monthly earnings for all respondents, men and women, of working age in employment.

3. Note that the cell sizes for self-employed women reporting earnings are small in some cases and so may not be reliable estimates.

4. Non-job specific training or education was defined as any which is not provided by or paid for by an employer or any that was not a requirement laid down by an employer. This means that non-job specific training could be aimed at developing employment skills but was undertaken by the respondent at their own cost or on a voluntary basis. Non-job specific training could therefore include government training schemes, Open University courses, correspondence courses and work experience schemes.

5. Respondents were asked to reply 'yes' or 'no' to each item. More than one reason for undertaking the training/education could therefore be given.

6. As with non-job specific training respondents could specify more than one reason for undertaking the training.

7. Note: a t-test comparing the mean days spent on training for all highly qualified and lower qualified showed statistically significant differences for both types of training at <.001.

8. Note that 'not in employment' includes the unemployed and the economically inactive.

9. The cell sizes for these movements in and out of paid employment are relatively small so may not be an accurate estimate in all cases.

10. If respondents did not feel the item applied to them in their current job the response was coded zero.

11. 'Childcare' includes those who said they were caring for young children, older children childcare in general, and pregnancy.

    'Other family care' includes general family care, care of spouse/partner, family obligations.

    'Other' includes care of other relatives/parents, divorce/separation, ill health, financial/family business and other responses.

    The numbers in these categories were relatively small so have not been listed separately.

12. The tables on attitudes should be interpreteted with care due to the relatively small cell sizes in some cases.

Conclusion

This analysis using 1991 BHPS data has highlighted some key features relating to the position of highly qualified women in the labour market. Overall, it found that higher qualified women do better in the labour market than less qualified women but that when compared to men with similar qualifications, men still apparently do better than women.

Many of the higher status occupations which demand higher levels of qualifications for entry, show distinct gender imbalances. Although, patterns of female employment in the professions showed a significant rate of growth during the 1970's and 1980s, data from the BHPS reveals that men still dominate the science and engineering sectors of the professional job market, with women continuing to choose teaching and nursing occupations. This suggests that equal opportunities policies and incentives aimed to attract women into these traditionally male dominated sectors of the labour market may have had only limited success.

In addition to segregation in the labour market, which is evident even in highly qualified women's jobs, the marked inequality in pay from employment suggests that women with equivalent qualifications to men, are continuing to suffer a 'ceiling effect'.

Bibliography

Barron, K.D. and Norris, G.M. (1976) 'Sexual Divisions and the Dual Labour Market', in D.L. Barker and S. Allen (eds.) (1976) *Dependence and Exploitation in Work and Marriage*. London: Longman.

Crompton, R. and Sanderson, K. (1990) *Gendered Jobs and Social Change*. London: Unwin Hyman.

Dale, A. and Glover, J. (1990) *An Analysis of Women's Employment Patterns in the UK, France and the USA*, Research Paper No. 75. London: Department of Employment.

Dex, S. (1985) *The Sexual Division of Work*. Brighton: Wheatsheaf.

Dex, S. (1987) *Women's Occupational Mobility: A Lifetime Perspective*. London: Macmillan.

Dex, S. (1992) 'Labour Force Participation of Women During the 1990's: Occupational mobility and part-time employment', in R. M. Lindley (ed.) *Womens Employment: Britain and the Single European Market. Research Series*, Equal Opportunities Commission, London: HMSO.

Dolton, P.J. and Makepeace, G.H (1992) *The Early Careers of 1980 Graduates: Work Histories, Job Tenure, Career Mobility and Occupational Choice*, Research Paper No.79. London: Department of Employment.

General Household Survey (1987). London: HMSO.

Institute for Employment Research (1992) *Review of the Economy and Employment, Occupational Studies, Managerial, Professional and Technical Occupations*. University of Warwick.

Martin, J. and Roberts, C. (1984) *Women and Employment: A Lifetime Perspective*. London: HMSO.

Novarra, V. (1980) *Women's Work, Men's Work*. London: Marion Boyars.

Skills and Enterprise Network (1993) 'Giving Women Equal Access to Training' Skills and Enterprise Network, Employment Department Group, Nottingham

Standard Occupational Classification (SOC) Volume 3 (1990). London: OPCS.

Appendix A

The definition of sub-major groups and constituent minor groups

Appendix A

D17. **SHOWCARD D3**
Please look at this card. Do you have any of the qualifications listed?

27

Yes ------------------ 1 **ASK D18**
No ------------------ 2 **GO TO D19**

D18. Which qualifications do you have?

CODE ALL THAT APPLY

a) Youth training certificate ------------------------------------- 01   28-29

b) Recognised trade apprenticeship completed -------------------- 02   30-31

c) Clerical and commercial qualifications
    (eg typing/shorthand/book-keeping/commerce) ----------- 03   32-33

d) City & Guilds Certificate -
    Craft/Intermediate/Ordinary/Part I -------------------- 04   34-35

e) City & Guilds Certificate - Advanced/Final/Part II ---------- 05   36-37

f) City & Guilds Certificate - Full Technological/Part III ----- 06   38-39

g) Ordinary National Certificate (ONC) or Diploma (OND),
    BEC/TEC/BTEC National/General Certificate or Diploma -- 07   40-41

h) Higher National Certificate (HNC) or Diploma (HND),
    BEC/TEC/BTEC Higher Certificate or Higher Diploma ----- 08   42-43

i) Nursing qualifications (eg SEN, SRN, SCM) -------------------- 09   44-45

j) Teaching qualifications (not degree) ------------------------ 10   46-47

k) University diploma -- 11   48-49

l) University or CNAA First Degree (eg BA, B.Ed, BSc) ---------- 12   50-51

m) University or CNAA Higher Degree (eg MSc, PhD) -------------- 13   52-53

n) Other technical, professional or higher qualifications

    (SPECIFY) _____ 14   54-55

Appendix B

Appendix B

The Definition of Sub-major Groups and Constituent Minor Groups

Major Group	Sub-major Groups	Constituent Minor Groups
1 Managers and Administrators	a) Corporate Managers and Administrators	10,11,12,13,14,15,19
	b) Managers/Proprietors in Agriculture and Services	16,17
2 Professional Occupations	a) Science and Engineering Professionals	20,21
	b) Health Professionals	22
	c) Teaching Professionals	23
	d) Other Professional Occupations	24,25,26,27,29
3 Associate Professional and Technical Occupations	a) Science and Engineering Associate Professionals	30,31,32
	b) Health Associate Professionals	34
	c) Other Associate Professional Occupations	33,35,36,37,38,39
4 Clerical and Secretarial Occupations	a) Clerical Occupations	40,41,42,43,44,49
	b) Secretarial Occupations	45,46
5 Craft and Related Occupations	a) Skilled Construction Trades	50
	b) Skilled Engineering Trades	51,52
	c) Other Skilled Trades	53,54,55,56,57,58,59
6 Personal and Protective Service Occupations	a) Protective Service Occupation	60,61
	b) Personal Service Occupations	62,63,64,65,66,67,69
7 Sales Occupations	a) Buyers, Brokers and Sales Reps	70,71
	b) Other Sales Occupations	72,73,79
8 Plant and Machine Operatives	a) Industrial Plant and Machine Operators, Assemblers	80,81,82,83,84,85,86,89
	b) Drivers and Mobile Machine Operators	87,88
9 Other Occupations	a) Other Occupations in Agriculture, Forestry and Fishing	90
	b) Other Elementary Occupations	91,92,93.94,95,99

SOURCE: SOC Vol 1, OPCS, HMSO 1990.

Appendix C

Appendix C

General Nature of Qualifications, Training and Experience for Occupations in SOC Major Groups

Major Group	General Nature of Qualifications, Training and Experience for Occupations in the Major Group
Managers and Administrators	A significant amount of knowledge and experience of the production processes, administrative procedures or service requirements associated with the efficient functioning of organisations and businesses.
Professional Occupations	A degree or equivalent qualification, with some occupations requiring post graduate qualifications and/or a formal period of experience-related training.
Associate Professional and Technical Occupations	An associated high-level vocational qualification, often involving a substantial period of full-time training or further study. Some additional task-related training is usually provided through a formal period of induction.
Clerical and Secretarial Occupations	A good standard of general education. Certain occupations will require further additional vocational training to a well defined standard (eg typing or shorthand).
Craft and Related Occupations	A substantial period of training, often provided by means of a work-based training programme.
Personal and Protective Service Occupations	A good standard of general education. Certain occupations will require further additional vocational training, often provided by means of a work-based training programme.
Sales Occupations	A general education and a programme of work-based training related to sales procedures. Some occupations require additional specific technical knowledge but are included in this major group because the primary task involves selling.
Plant and Machine Operatives	The knowledge and experience necessary to operate vehicles and other mobile and stationary machinery, to operate and monitor industrial plant and equipment, to assemble products from component parts according to strict rules and procedures and subject assembled parts to routine tests. Most occupations in this major group will specify a minimum standard of competence that must be attained for satisfactory performance of the associated tasks and will have an associated period of formal experience-related training.
Other Occupations	The knowledge and experience necessary to perform mostly simple and routine tasks involving the use of hand-held tools and in some cases, requiring a degree of physical effort. Most occupations in the major group require no formal educational qualifications but will usually have an associated short period of formal experienced-related training. All non-managerial agricultural occupations are also included in this major group, primarily because of the difficulty of distinguishing between those occupations which require only a limited knowledge of agricultural techniques, animal husbandry, etc from those which require specific training and experience in these areas. These occupations are defined in a separate minor group.

SOURCE: SOC Vol 1, OPCS, HMSO 1990

EMPLOYMENT DEPARTMENT
RESEARCH SERIES

The Research Series of reports was introduced in March 1992 and supersedes the Department's Research Papers (covering employment and industrial relations issues) and the Training Research and Development series.

Listed below are the current reports in the new series. Copies can be obtained free of charge from Research Management Branch, Employment Department, Room W441, Moorfoot, Sheffield S1 4PQ or by contacting our Orderline telephone number 0114 259-3932.

Listings of Research Papers and Training Research and Development reports can be obtained by contacting the above address or telephone number.

RES

No.   Title and author(s)

1. **Measure for Measure**

   A comparative analysis of measures to combat racial discrimination in the member states of the European Community. I Forbes and G Mead, Equal Opportunities Study Group, University of Southampton. 1992.

2. **New Developments in Employee Involvement**

   M Marchington, J Goodman, A Wilkinson and P Ackers, Manchester School of Management, UMIST. 1992.

3. **Entrepreneurship in Cleveland 1979-1989: A Study of the Effects of the Enterprise Culture**

   D J Storey and A Strange, Centre for Small and Medium Sized Enterprises, Warwick Business School, University of Warwick. 1992.

4. **Alcohol Consumption and Sickness Absence: An Analysis of 1984 General Household Survey Data.**

   L M Joeman, Employment Department. 1992.

5. **Payment Systems: A Look at Current Practices.**

   B Casey, J Lakey and M White, Policy Studies Institute. September 1992.

6. **New Inward Investment and the Northern Region Labour Market.**

   F Peck and I Stone, Newcastle Economic Research Unit, University of Northumbria at Newcastle. October 1992.

7. **Final-Offer Arbitration in the UK: Incidence, processes and outcomes.**

   S Milner, Centre for Economic Performance, London School of Economics. January 1993.

8. **Information Requirements in Occupational Decision Making**

   Dr N C Boreham and Dr T A A Arthur, University of Manchester. March 1993.

9. **The Motivation to Train**

   M Crowder and K Pupynin, Minds at Work. April 1993.

10. **TEC Participation in National Development Activity**

    Ernst & Young. May 1993.

11. Business Growth Training Option 3 Evaluation Project

   J. Neill Marshall, Neil Alderman, Cecilia Wong and Alfred Thwaites, Centre for Urban and Regional Development Studies, University of Newcastle.   May 1993.

12. TECs & employers: Developing effective links. Part 1: a survey.

   Patrick Vaughan, Employment Department. July 1993.

13. TECs & employers: Developing effective links. Part 2: TEC-employer links in six TEC areas.

   Theresa Crowley-Bainton, Policy Studies Institute. August 1993.

14. The Abolition of the Dock Labour Scheme.

   N Evans and D MacKay, Pieda plc and M Garratt and P Sutcliffe, MDS Transmodal. September 1993.

15. New firm formation and small business growth in the United Kingdom: Spatial and temporal variations and determinants

   D Keeble and S Walker, Department of Geography and Small Business Research Centre, University of Cambridge, and M Robson, Department of Economics, University of Newcastle-upon-Tyne. September 1993.

16. Employment Policies for Disabled People: A review of legislation and services in fifteen countries

   N Lunt and P Thornton, Social Policy Research Unit, University of York. October 1993.

17. An Evaluation of Supported Employment Initiatives for Disabled People

   A Pozner and J Hammond, OUTSET Consultancy Services (with a contribution by V Tannam, Employment Service). October 1993.

18. Teleworking in Britain

   Ursula Huws, Analytica. October 1993.

19. Partnerships for Equality: A review of Employers' Equal Opportunities Groups

   G Whitting, J Moore and P Warren, ECOTEC Research and Consulting Ltd. October 1993.

20. Factors Influencing Individual Committment to Lifetime Learning

   Malcolm Maguire, Susan Maguire and Alan Felstead, Centre for Labour Market Studies, University of Leicester. December 1993.

21. Investors in People. A qualitative study of employers.

   A Rix, R Parkinson and R Gaunt, CRG People at Work. January 1994.

22. The 1992 Survey of Industrial Tribunal Applications

   Nigel Tremlett, Social and Community Planning Research (SCPR) and Nitya Banerji, Employment Department. February 1994.

23. Thinking and Learning at Work: A report on the development and evaluation of the Thinking Skills At Work modules

   Nigel Blagg, Rachel Lewis and Marj Ballinger, Nigel Blagg Associates. March 1994.

24. The Early Use of Local Initiative Funds by TECs: Evoking local prosperity

   John Bazalgette, David Armstrong, Jean Hutton and Colin Quine, The Grubb Institute. March 1994.

25. Regional Advice Units: An examination of models for delivering advice and guidance to TECs and Department of Employment Regional Offices

   Kate Pupynin and Mary Crowder, Minds at Work. April 1994.

26. The Role of Evaluation in TEC Planning: Final report

   Ian Pearson, WMEB Consultants. April 1994.

27. The Changing Structure of Occupations and Earnings in Great Britain, 1975-1990. An analysis based on the New Earnings Survey Panel Dataset.

   P Elias and M Gregory, Institute for Employment Research, University of Warwick. May 1994.

28. Middle Managers: Their Contribution to Employee Involvement

   M Fenton O'Creevy and N Nicholson, Centre for Organisational Research, London Business School. June 1994.

29. **An International Overview of Employment Policies and Practices Towards Older Workers**

J Moore, B Tilson and G Whitting, ECOTEC Research and Consulting Ltd. June 1994.

30. **Training: An exploration of the word and the concept with an analysis of the implications for survey design**

P Campanelli with Roger Thomas, Survey Methods Centre, SCPR, and J Channell with L McAulay and A Renouf, Research & Development Unit for English Studies, University of Birmingham. July 1994.

31. **Individual Commitment to Lifetime Learning: Individuals' Attitudes. Report on the qualitative phase.**

S Taylor and L Spencer, Social and Community Planning Research (SCPR). July 1994.

32. **Individual Commitment to Lifetime Learning: Individuals' Attitudes. Report on the quantitative survey.**

A Park, Social and Community Planning Research (SCPR). July 1994.

33. **Sunday Working. Analysis of an Employer Survey.**

Prof. D Bosworth, Manchester School of Management, UMIST. August 1994.

34. **The Economic Effects of Reductions in Working Hours: the UK Engineering Industry.**

R Richardson and M Rubin, Department of Industrial Relations and Centre for Economic Performance, London School of Economics. September 1994.

35. **Participation and Progress in the Labour Market: Key issues for women.**

L Spencer and S Taylor, Social and Community Planning Research (SCPR). September 1994.

36. **Acting Positively: Positive action under the Race Relations Act 1976.**

C Welsh, J Knox and M Brett, Capita Management Consultancy. October 1994.

37. **The Impact of the Posted Workers' Directive on Company Practice in the United Kingdom.**

M Gold, National Institute of Economic and Social Research. October 1994.

38. **Thematic Evaluation of EHEI.**

C Biggs, R Brighton, P Minnitt, R Pow and W Wicksteed, Segal Quince Wicksteed Ltd. October 1994.

39. **Caring and Employment**

L Corti, H Laurie and S Dex, ESRC Research Centre on Micro-social Change, University of Essex. November 1994.

40. **Individual Commitment to Learning: Employers' Attitudes**

H Metcalf, A Walling and M Fogarty, Policy Studies Institute. November 1994.

41. **Employment and Family Life: A review of research in the UK (1980-1994)**

J Brannen, G Mészáros, P Moss and G Poland, Centre for Research on Family Life and Employment, Thomas Coram Research Unit, Institute of Education, University of London. November 1994.

42. **Individual Commitment to Learning: Individuals' Decision-Making About 'Lifetime Learning'**

A Hand, J Gambles and E Cooper, Quadrangle Consulting Ltd. November 1994.

43. **Household Labour Supply**

S Dex, A Clark and M Taylor, ESRC Research Centre on Micro-social Change, University of Essesx. January 1995.

44. **The Out-of-School Childcare Grant Initiative: An interim evaluation**

I Sanderson and J Percy-Smith, with A Foreman, M Wraight and L Murphy, Policy Research Unit, Leeds Metropolitan University and P Petrie, Thomas Coram Research Unit, University of London. January 1995.

45. **Evaluation of the Open Learning Credits Pilot Programme: Summary report**

T Crowley-Bainton, Policy Studies Institute. January 1995.

46. **TECS and their Non-Employer Stakeholders**

G Haughton, T Hart, I Strange and K Thomas, CUDEM, School of the Environment, Leeds Metropolitan University, and J Peck, SPA, School of Geography, Manchester University. February 1995.

47. **Individual Commitment to Learning:**
    Providers' attitudes

    N Tremlett, A Thomas and S Taylor, Social and
    Community Planning Research (SCPR). March
    1995.

48. **Labour Market Flexibility**

    M Beatson, Employment Market Research Unit,
    Employment Department. April 1995.

49. **The Exercise of Individual Employment Rights**
    in the Member States of the European
    Community

    C Barnard, J Clark and R Lewis, University of
    Southampton. April 1995.

50. **Highly Qualified Women**

    L Corti, H Laurie and S Dex, ESRC Research
    Centre on Micro-social Change, University of
    Essex. April 1995.